TALES FROM THE
CITY

TALES FROM THE
CITY

A collection of writing inspired
by Norwich City Football Club

Volume Two
Edited by Mick Dennis

TALES FROM
www.talesfrom.com

First published in Great Britain in 2016
by Tales From

Printed and bound by SS Media

Cover photography by www.stonecreativedesign.com

ISBN 978-0-9932381-3-0

Tales From Ltd
107 Jupiter Drive, Hemel Hempstead, Herts HP2 5NU
Registered company number: 9082738

www.talesfrom.com
info@talesfrom.com

TALES FROM THE CITY

CONTENTS

INTRODUCTION

BY THE EDITOR

Queens Park Rangers fans don't like me. Newcastle supporters don't send me Christmas cards either. Chelsea fans trolled me into quitting Twitter for a fortnight. If you make a living by expressing strident opinions about football, as I did for a long time, you are bound to upset people. I was seldom bothered by the flak because I never wrote anything I didn't believe.

I hate it when Norwich fans abuse me though. It hasn't happened very often, but it is tough to take. It's like a family row.

I remember an incident at Cardiff on February 1, 2014, in Chris Hughton's last season as manager. Robert Snodgrass gave Norwich the lead after only five minutes, the Canaries played some good stuff, and it all looked very encouraging. Then, just four minutes into the second half, they conceded twice within 60 seconds – and I saw this bloke forcing his way along to where I was standing with two close friends. I knew straight away that he was coming to have a go at me. I'd never had a conversation with him before, as far as I could recall, but his face was contorted with fury and, as he shoved his way along the row, I knew he intended to use me as an excuse to vent his anger.

'Do you STILL support Hootun?' he shouted into my face.

'Mate, I'm hurting too', I replied.

'What the eff did he say to them at half-time?'

'Well I don't suppose he said to Gary Hooper, "Slap a silly

pass across the face of your own area so that they can get a goal." Do you?'

I always use that 'I'm hurting too' line, because it is true. None of us enjoys watching Norwich lose.

When I assembled the first volume of *Tales From The City*, the euphoria of the play-off final win over Middlesbrough was a motivation. This time, a dismal demotion has occurred. I watched one critical defeat – by Sunderland at our place – on my mobile phone in the recovery area of an operating theatre after surgery. At 0-0, Norwich conceded a penalty. I yelled, 'No!' And a crowd of worried people in scrubs rushed to my bedside.

My recovery wasn't helped by the next few matches but on the night relegation was confirmed, Jonathan Liew's report for *The Telegraph* captured the mood at Carrow Road: 'Norwich went down, but they went down singing. There was defiance on the pitch as they produced one of their best performances of the season; there was defiance off it as their fans toasted a fourth Premier League relegation with a chorus of song. "Ipswich Town, we're coming for you," they roared, all of a sudden relishing the prospect of renewing parochial rivalries. After that one ended, they broke out "City till I die". The noise split the ears and warmed the heart. In those 45 minutes, Norwich's fans reminded everyone that the best thing about supporting a football team is not winning, but belonging.'

So welcome to *Tales From The City* Volume 2 – in which 11 people I admire give insights into the life of the club we care about.

You will find some recurring themes. Several writers mention the end of Robert Chase's tenure as chairman. Four talk about the time when Ron Saunders was replaced as manager by John Bond. Two highlight the 2003-04 season, when Norwich topped the Football League. And so, by presenting different perspectives, I hope this book provides a rounded view of big moments in the history of our club.

Several of the tales in this book have dark passages. One deals with racism and another with depression. But in an entirely different tone, one of the club's all-time greats recounts his extraordinary career in the most understated, matter-of-fact manner possible.

Again, my hope is that these very varied, human stories help create a more complete understanding of how our club has been shaped and of the people who have shaped it.

Our lowest ebb for half a century was the 7-1 home defeat by Colchester with which Norwich started life in the third tier in August 2009. Three days later came a League Cup tie at Yeovil. Norwich won 4-0, with a new signing – some chap called Grant Holt – scoring a hat-trick. Wesley Hoolahan scored the other one. Perhaps we should have made a song about that game.

But it wasn't events on the field that cheered me. At Huish Park before kick off, in the car park behind the away end, the Yellow Army had mustered: battered by events, wearied by the journey but defiantly loyal. There was a lot of gallows humour, but it was an utterly magnificent demonstration of unbreakable allegiance by 1,000 supporters who travelled 250 miles so soon after a crushingly dismal weekend.

I understand why, in defeat, some people get angry. But we're all in this together. And that is a glorious thing. I'm sure you understand. If you are reading this book, you're almost certainly a fan of the great club from the fine city and so you and I share a passion and a bond. It is my fervent desire that this book enriches the enjoyment you get from your commitment to Norwich City.

Mick Dennis

1

When he was leading the club's goal charts year after year, he was a Norwich City hero. Now he works as a teaching assistant.

Robert Fleck insists we should not be surprised about his new calling, but his tale is full of revelations. There is real sadness, an admission and a full explanation of how he found fulfilment away from the game and the goals.

MY JOURNEY TO SCHOOL

BY ROBERT FLECK

I don't know why people were surprised when it was reported that I work as a classroom assistant at a school for children with complex needs. Why is it surprising? Because I was a footballer? But footballers are just human beings. I would say 99 per cent of footballers give money to charity, or go into schools and hospitals without being asked and without people knowing. They don't do it for publicity and they don't want publicity about it.

Football was a big part of my life: a hobby that I was lucky enough to get paid well for. But there came a time when it was over and I just had to get on with the rest of my life. And now my working life is at Parkside School in Norwich. I seldom talk about the football part now, and don't often give interviews, but the fact that Dave Stringer was contributing to this book made me think, 'If it's good enough for him…'

Dave was the manager who signed me for Norwich from Glasgow Rangers in December and became like a father to me in some ways. But the first game I played for Norwich was such a shock that I flew home to Scotland and told people I wasn't going back south again.

I had known about the Norwich interest for some time. Chris Woods, the Rangers goalkeeper, had been at Norwich and so I spoke about the club and the city long and hard to Chris and his wife. They sold the idea of going to Carrow Road to me.

But Leeds and Newcastle were interested as well and I had talks with Dave Bassett, the manager at Watford. He was offering more money than Norwich, but something didn't feel right when I spoke to him. He more or less said I was his last throw of the dice. I thought, 'Hold on. If the last throw doesn't work, I'm going to get the flak and the next manager might want to get rid of me.' I was 22 years of age and if I was going to play in England I wanted to be at a club with some stability.

On the Tuesday evening, a few days after I'd spoken with Watford, I played for Rangers against Dunfermline at Ibrox. There were 36,000 people there and they were singing for me not to leave, but after the game I was told Norwich had come to sign me. I talked to Dave Stringer and the chairman, Robert Chase, and the next morning I was on a flight with them to Norwich.

That was the Wednesday. On the Friday we played Wimbledon at Plough Lane and seven or eight of my friends came down to watch. The crowd was just over 4,000. It was a bit different from Ibrox just three nights before. I had been to some bad places in my time in Glasgow but Plough Lane was the worst. It was awful and Norwich lost 1-0. I flew back to Scotland for the weekend and said, 'I am not going back south.'

My dad said, 'You are not a quitter and you are not going to quit now. Go back and make the most of it'. So I went back to Norwich.

I was a single lad and I stayed with Bryan Gunn for three months while I had a house built. In those three months, I think he cooked once. We went out every night and there would be a toss of the coin to see who would buy dinner. He only paid about once. I checked his coin all the time, but he kept winning the toss.

It was okay for players to go out in Norwich. As with every club at that time, there was alcohol involved. We worked hard

– boy, did we work hard at training and on the pitch – but we played hard as well. That was the culture at the time but nobody got into any trouble. We knew where we could go and where not to go and I can't remember anyone getting into fights or arguments or anything.

I was a lucky man. My face fitted at most of the clubs I went to and I think that, sometimes, if your face fits you get the job. There were kids who were better than me but got released by Glasgow Rangers. I wasn't the most gifted of footballers, but coming from a working class family in Glasgow, you had to work hard to get what you had, and so I had a work ethic.

My attitude was that I would go out and show the club that I was working for that I would give as much as I could: running about, trying to win the ball, trying to get it back if you lost it, trying to get goals and – instead of walking back or getting frustrated – always running from the opposition half to get back.

It was just a working class thing. And I knew it was what the fans wanted to see because I'd been a fan myself. As a kid I had paid to watch Glasgow Rangers play. I knew what it was like to pay good money to watch football, and I knew the fans were the people who were paying my wages, so I thought I had to give something back.

At Rangers I had played under John Greig, Jock Wallace and Graeme Souness: all men who respected hard work. Then, when I got to Norwich, Dave Stringer was a man from a working background and so it wasn't hard for me to give everything in training and practice games to say, 'This is what I am about'.

I had been quite fortunate with the players I played alongside at Glasgow Rangers. I had Trevor Francis, Ray Wilkins, Graham Roberts, Terry Butcher, Ally McCoist, Souness and people like that. But Norwich played the sort of football I like as well. When I got there, Bryan Gunn was in goal and we had Ian Culverhouse, Ian Crook, Mark Bowen, Dale Gordon and

Ruel Fox: intelligent players, and a team who wanted to play football instead of humping it and running.

They made me feel very welcome, so it was quite easy to fit in. Up front with me was Robert Rosario. He was the most unselfish player I ever played alongside and he didn't get the credit for what he did. In fact he took a lot of criticism, but he was fantastic to have in the dressing room and on the pitch. Fans make quick judgements sometimes and I thought the criticism was unfair.

My first Norwich goal was against Manchester United, and that would be one of my highlights. It was at Carrow Road and it was against a team whose fans didn't like me because they align themselves with Celtic. So it gave me great pleasure to score that goal.

People seem to remember the winner at Millwall, in my first full season: 1988-89. It was a Sunday game and was live on ITV and, from my point of view, it was one of the most exciting matches I have ever been involved in.

We were 2-0 up in the first seven minutes, both from Dale Gordon corners. The first was from the left. I got my head to it to flick it on and Ian Butterworth scored at the far post with a shot. The second corner, from the right, was cleared but Andy Linighan hit a shot that was saved. I got to the rebound and turned the ball to Robert Rosario. His shot hit somebody and ricocheted to Mark Bowen who tapped it in. They got two back before half-time, and Gunny had a phenomenal game as we came under pressure. He was definitely man-of-the-match, although on TV Ian St John gave it to a Millwall player.

My winner came in time added on. It was a volley on the half-turn from the edge of the penalty box. My legs were really tired, but fortunately the ball went over the goalkeeper's head.

During my time at Norwich under Dave Stringer the two FA Cup semi-finals we reached stood out – but definitely not for good reasons. In 1989, on the day before our semi-final against Everton at Villa Park, I spoke to my dad on the phone after lunch and some of the boys had gone out but I was just relaxing in the hotel. Then, at about four o'clock, there was a big bang on my door and it was the gaffer who wanted me to go and talk to him. We walked along the corridor and he looked so serious that I thought, 'If I am not playing tomorrow I am going home'.

I couldn't think of anything else he would want to talk to me about other than that for some reason he was going to leave me out for the semi-final. But then he told me it was bad news. My dad, John, had died, aged 46. He'd had a heart attack, not that long after I had spoken to him on the phone.

My first thought was for my mum. I phoned her and said, 'Right I'm on the first flight up to you'. She told me I should stay and play but I wanted to be with her. It was when I was on the plane from Birmingham that I thought I should have stayed and played, just for my dad. The fact that I didn't is the one big regret I have about my football choices.

I spent the next day at home in Glasgow with my mum and my family. We knew Norwich had lost, but that was also the day when the Hillsborough disaster happened at the other semi-final, and that put football in perspective. But I do wish I had played for Norwich against Everton for my dad.

Three years later, we reached the semi-final again. I got my ribs broken by Glenn Cockerill of Southampton at our place in a quarter-final replay. It happened in the first five minutes but the doctor gave me an injection and I stayed on and then Matt Le Tissier got sent off for kicking me. We got through to the semi-final and I spent time in an oxygen chamber to help my recovery.

This time our semi-final was at Hillsborough, against Sunderland. I asked the gaffer if I could play in a reserve game on the Tuesday before we travelled for the semi. I needed a half-hour run out. But he said, 'No, because I want to make out you will not be fit for Saturday.' He was trying kidology.

I was desperate to play at Hillsborough, because I had missed the 1989 one and I thought I owed the fans, myself and my dad. I did play. It was one of my worst days in football. We were the better team and had chances to win the game. But John Byrne, who had scored in every round, got the only goal. It was my biggest heartbreak in football. I just sat by a post at the end and cried.

The defeat was crushing because, if I am honest, we all choked. We had been favourites but we didn't turn up. And the other reason it was crushing was that semi-finals had a connection in my mind with my dad.

I have some much happier memories. The most important goal I scored for Norwich was probably against Wimbledon, in April 1992. We were struggling and my goal gave us a 1-1 draw that more or less kept us up.

Throughout that period when Dave Stringer was manager we stayed in the top division and that was a great achievement for 'Little Norwich', as people wanted to keep calling us. We finished fourth one season.

The manager was such a gentle, lovable person. Dave Williams was first team coach, and very good, but Dave Stringer was the manager, and everyone knew where they stood.

In the team, we all knew what we had to do but we had a freedom to express ourselves within the system. The full backs were allowed to join in the attacks, for instance, because they knew full well that someone would cover for them. Everyone knows the goals that Mark Bowen scored over the years from left back for Norwich, which shows the sort of team we were, but he would have someone like Trevor Putney tucking in behind to cover.

There were thinkers in the team and all good footballers. Micky Phelan, for example, was great for us and then you think what he went on to achieve as a coach at Manchester United. It shows the calibre of person we had in the Norwich team.

We were all quick to let one another know if someone wasn't doing his job properly but there was never a case of anyone going in a huff or sulking. My attitude was that if someone told me I wasn't doing something, I would think, 'That must be right', and if I had to tell someone the response was the same. It was a good team spirit, a good bond, a good understanding.

As a manager, Dave would fight your corner, but if you did anything wrong you would know about it. He would certainly tell you. I think if anyone sat down with him for a talk, they would know that he was taking the job personally. He wanted to be a winner and he didn't want to let people down.

I scored that goal against Wimbledon that meant we were safe, and then, before the last game of the season, which was at Leeds, we found out that Dave was stepping down as manager. I was gutted because I thought he had a lot more to offer. But his decision was to stop, and he is a man who stands by his decisions.

Mike Walker took over and he tried to stamp his own authority on it, but I left that summer. I had nearly joined Chelsea the year before but for some reason it fell through but all through my last season in that first spell at Norwich I knew I would be leaving.

When I did, it gave Mike the money to go and buy Mark Robbins, who began with two goals at Arsenal and went on to prove what a good player and scorer he was.

It felt right for me to go to Chelsea because I'd been ready to do so a year before and I just felt I shouldn't go somewhere else because they were offering me £500 a week more. I did speak to Terry Venables at Tottenham the night before I signed for Chelsea, and other clubs were interested, but I had a gut feeling that it should be Chelsea. Back in November 1991, Norwich had beaten them 3-0 away and I had scored a couple of goals. The whole Shed End at Stamford Bridge applauded me and that had stayed in my head.

Ian Porterfield was the Chelsea manager when I joined them, in the summer of 1992, and Don Howe was his assistant manager. The records show that Chelsea wasn't my best spell, but they also show that in the first half of the season I went there I was top of the assists. Don Howe's coaching meant we were told to play as Arsenal had played under him. That meant 'defending from the front', and it was a completely different style to what I had been used to at Norwich.

Ian Porterfield got the sack and Dave Webb came in. He was as honest as the day is long. He said, 'If we get a bid for you Robert, we'll let you go, because I am going to play with two big men up front: Tony Cascarino and Mick Harford'.

Then Glenn Hoddle came in as manager and that's not worth talking about – except that he was the one who told me when Norwich came in for me. At first they wanted me on loan but I didn't really believe in going back. It wasn't about not wanting to play for Norwich again. If it had been any club I would still have thought, 'I shouldn't go back'.

Norwich first came in for me to return in the summer. They had been relegated and Martin O'Neill had been appointed manager. They went to Northern Ireland on a pre-season tour, and I went to see him at his hotel.

But another reason I wanted to stay at Chelsea was to mess Glenn about. I'd been out on loan at Bolton and Bristol and there had been a chance of me playing abroad, but he had messed that up, so I thought I would stay – because the longer I stayed the more it pissed him off.

Then I thought about it some more and decided I would

re-join Norwich. I didn't really want it to be on loan though. My wife, Jayne, was a Norwich girl and I didn't fancy getting my wife settled back in Norfolk and then have to leave again. So I said I would re-join Norwich if it would be a permanent move.

I'd had a problem with my right knee for about a year and the medical wasn't perfect. Tim Sheppard was the Norwich physio, and was a good friend. He said, 'If it was me buying him, I wouldn't do it'. But Martin signed me and the joy on my wife's face was a picture and made me sure it was the right decision.

Of course, Martin didn't hang around long. The players had a little inkling that things weren't right between him and the chairman, Mr Chase, because Martin wasn't himself. The chairman wouldn't give him the money to buy Dean Windass and Martin, being the proud man he is, said he would leave. If we had kept Martin there is not a shadow of doubt we would have got promoted that year.

There were demonstrations and protests about the chairman, but as a player you couldn't let that interfere with your football on the training ground or on the pitch. At the end of the day, the football was your job and you had to do it to the best of your ability.

But for me personally, and some of the others, because we got on so well with Mr Chase, we were disappointed about the protests. We felt that he was hard done by, when you think what was achieved when he was chairman at the club. He was fantastic for the players, too. But when results don't go well, supporters are going to take it out on someone: probably the manager or the chairman. And in this case it was the chairman.

In that second period for me at Norwich, I didn't play right up top. I played a little deeper, trying to link up play, but still get into the box. In the second tier you couldn't play the type of football we had played in the top division, and a lot of good players had moved on. Time had taken its toll on some, and confidence had gone as well.

I left Norwich for the second time when they sold me to Reading in March 1998, but at the end of the following season, I retired from the professional game because my back wasn't fit to keep going.

Dale Gordon was manager of Gorleston and Jimmy Jones, who had been on the Norwich board, was the chairman. Dale asked me to go along and help, and I said I would but I also said, 'Don't ever ask me to play because I am never going to'.

But in one game an opponent stamped on the head of our kid striker. I said, 'I bet you wouldn't do that to me'. He was giving it the big one back. So I said, 'The next time you play us I am going to hurt you like you hurt that kid'. So I got myself fit and in the team and I did play against him and I did hurt him: not too badly but just enough to make a point.

Dale left and Jimmy Jones, who I had got on well with when he was at Norwich, asked me to take over, which I did. The players were a great bunch of lads. They would be at work all day, and then get home, get changed and come training. It was back to the work ethic that I believed in and I thoroughly enjoyed it.

Next I went to Diss and was there for about three seasons, but I got the sack and I turned around and said to myself, 'Right, I am not going to another club. That was the first time I have been sacked but it will be the last time I am sacked too'.

From that moment I have had no contact with local football.

I think I am lucky that my wife doesn't like football. I have seen footballers' wives in the players' bar after a game talking as if they were the manager and telling their husbands what they've done wrong. With Jayne, I'd go home and tell her we'd won and she would say, 'Well done'. Or I would tell her we'd lost and she would say, 'Oh, not to worry'.

I would sit on my own in a room for an hour to calm down but, after that, Jayne would say, 'Robert, come on, it's family time again'. I was also lucky that I had friends outside the football as well. I can't pretend there weren't a few dark days when I first stopped playing, but because of Jayne I had a home life that didn't include football and I was able to move on. Because of how it had always been with Jayne, and some of our friends, I was able to say, 'What has gone has gone and it is time to get on with the rest of my life'.

I went back to thinking that football had been a hobby and that I had been really fortunate. I had international caps and medals and had got a hell of a lot out of my hobby. I did some scouting for Norwich, and enjoyed that, but eventually gave up even that.

I still don't take my work home to Jayne now. I don't really speak to her about what happens at the school. There are some things I am not allowed to speak about anyway. But I don't talk about it because she would find some of it upsetting.

I used to hire the school's hall to put on soccer schools on Wednesday evenings. I got to know the staff and got to know the set-up and they asked if I would do a day with their kids, who have special needs, in the summer. As a thank you for letting me use their hall, I did it. Obviously they must have seen that I was doing well with the kids, and a teacher there came up to me and told me there was a job going if I would be interested in applying for it. I thought, 'Why not?' It was the first interview I'd ever had for a job and I was really nervous, but thankfully it ended with me being taken on.

It is very rewarding. I'd say to anyone who thinks about getting involved at a school like Parkside, you will enjoy it, that's for sure. There are two teaching assistants in my class, some classes have three assistants and some have one. It depends on the needs of the children.

Every day is different. We could have young kids kicking off, biting you, kicking you or swearing at you. Obviously we have a word and get them back on the right road, and then when they come in the next morning you forget about the day before and it is a fresh start for them. We never hang on to what happened yesterday.

It is about getting to know the children and getting on with them. In the upper school, which is the years nine, ten and 11, the classes have mixed ages in them. That is something we started three or four years ago. Mine is an upper school class. I like working with the older children: helping them towards adulthood, helping them to go out into the big wide world.

We give the children breakfast in the morning and lunch later. We help them with putting clothes on, because they can't do it. We do everything. But we interact with them too and so we see them smile. If you don't feel good when you see a kid smile, there is something wrong with you. Whatever their difficulties, these kids have good hearts and have all got fun in them somewhere. We find how to get it out.

Russell Martin has been in two or three times. Wes Hoolahan donated some football tops to the school. It's the sort of thing lots of footballers do, but the school were really grateful. Football has a great power to grab people and get them interested and, as I said at the start, footballers are humans who respond as humans when there is something they can do to help someone else.

And I would say to footballers who want to give something back, when you retire go to a little school like the one I work in and try volunteering for a few hours a week. It will bring you back to earth and show you that football is not the be-all and end-all. It makes you think of what you have got, not what you haven't got.

When I first came down to Norwich, I got involved with helping a boy who was 15. Someone told me they were doing a sponsored walk for this boy who hadn't got long to live. I did the walk and then did other things. It touched my heart. Unfortunately he did die less than two years later, and I kept in touch with his mum and brother for a while.

I was lucky that I was running about but some of these kids have such a short lifespan. It wasn't something I would really speak about at the time. It was just something personal that I did. I mention it now because there are plenty of footballers who do understand how lucky they are and how unfortunate some other people are.

When I arrived in Norwich as a 22-year-old, and had that game at Plough Lane, I could not have imagined that when I packed up football I would settle in Norwich. And a couple of years later, when I was still at Norwich, Ian Porterfield was manager of Aberdeen and he tried to take me back to Scotland. But I had promised my dad and myself that I would stick it out in England, and give it a right good go. So that is what I did.

Robert Fleck was leading scorer for four consecutive seasons for Norwich and player of the year in 1992. He had two spells at the club, making more than 250 appearances and scoring 84 times. He played for Scotland in the 1990 World Cup and managed both Gorleston and Diss Town to victories in Norfolk Senior Cup finals.

2

Keith Skipper has championed Norfolk, its dialect and its ways all his working life.

When he reported on Norwich City, he revered the role and had a very clear idea what it should entail and what could not be tolerated.

Two very different managers, Ron Saunders and John Bond, presented contrasting challenges, and so this tale provides a unique perspective on a time of great drama and change.

A BEESTON BOY, THE HARD MAN
AND THE SHOWMAN

BY KEITH SKIPPER

I am sorely tempted to call up that grand old commentator Charles 'Early Doors' Dickens as summariser for my eventful seasons as a full-time Canary scribe. Then again, 'It was the best of times, it was the worst of times' scarcely embraces the complexities and intrigues of a period when football reporting should have carried a health warning for anyone daft enough to strike an individual pose.

Yes, my tale of one city and two managers of starkly contrasting character, Ron 'Gradgrind' Saunders and John 'Micawber' Bond, includes glamour, excitement and genuine pride in the rich achievements of a club I had loved and followed since childhood.

Yes, there were occasions when I had to temper a fiercely parochial spirit with a drop or two of chilling honesty so as to stay true to myself, and to thousands of devoted Norwich City supporters who had reason to trust what they read in the local newspapers.

Yes, I could have settled for an easier life, especially during the Saunders era, by constantly espousing the Carrow Road party line and 'looking on the bright side' whenever problems mounted amid poor results or weak displays.

But no, I do not regret my insistence on reflecting public opinion rather than trying to sway it. I saw my role, a very privileged one, as an unbiased reporter, not a passionate supporter. I survived with my notebook, pencil and principles – and some of my sanity – intact. Even so, it took an iron will and innate belief in real freedom of the press to keep going for the best part of a decade.

It's worth placing my reporting years in some sort of general context. When I kicked off, with the arrival of Ron Saunders in 1969, much of the nation still basked in the World Cup glory of Alf Ramsey and co. Many Canary fans still clung to the romance of that breathtaking 1958-59 FA Cup run ending so close to Wembley. There had been an outstanding Cup victory since over Manchester United at Old Trafford but nostalgia appeared a more potent force than faith in the future.

Local correspondents could get very close to clubs they were covering, particularly those outside the top flight, but I eschewed the growing habit of overloading match reports and reflective articles with fatuous quotes from manager or players. Nor did I repeat tittle-tattle from the national press… an occasional grain of wholesome wheat in a mountain of speculative chaff.

Remember, too, how Norwich's geographical position and 'country cousins' tag left them untroubled by Fleet Street newshounds for long periods before the club began rubbing shoulders with the big boys on a more regular basis.

Running reports in the *Pink Un* on Saturdays (when long queues still waited to read all about it at tea time) and in-depth Monday analysis in the *Eastern Daily Press* and *Evening News* dominated coverage. There was no local radio, no websites, and no blessed social media to spread facts, opinions and rumours. Television interest was largely confined to Anglia's *Match of the Week* highlights after Sunday lunch.

One of the biggest challenges of my Carrow Road tenure was acclimatising to a marked change in managerial personality and style about halfway through. Mr Saunders, dour and dogmatic, gave way to Mr Bond, all colour and controversy.

While one threw a protective shield around his players and confined himself to startling comments along 'We gave 110 per cent' lines, the other courted the media shamelessly and encouraged everyone within reach to wear bleeding hearts on sleeves.

They had nothing in common other than being born within a few weeks of each other in 1932, but both left to join Manchester City, further their careers and leave Norwich with the sort of 'stepping stone' complex Paul Lambert reinforced in more modern times.

I had served a long apprenticeship as aspiring soccer scribe on local club touchlines all over the area, covering Eastern Counties League, Anglian Combination, Norfolk Senior Cup, FA Amateur Cup, FA Sunday Cup and a host of junior competitions, before taking over from Dick Scales as Canary correspondent for the *Evening News* in Norwich.

He told me straight. 'This is one of the best jobs in the business. But it's also one of the hardest because it's impossible to keep everybody happy. You need a thick skin, a good sense of humour and unwavering belief in your own opinions.'

Dick might have added it could help to be over six feet tall, weigh in at a trim 14 stone and carry a cynical swagger made fashionable by Philip Marlowe on the means streets of Los Angeles. Oh, and to take the private eye analogy a step further, the knack of extracting vital information by phone had to be part of the armoury.

Even the most ardent believer in a manager's right to defend his kingdom in any way he sees fit had to admit it was hardly a fair fight when I was in the ring – the scrawny lad from Beeston (that's the real one between Dereham and Swaffham) up against the hard man from Birkenhead (that's the only one running along the west bank of the River Mersey). I am proud to say I survived four years of regular buffeting, occasional bullying and one period of complete banishment.

Saunders was City's tenth manager since the Second World War and by far the highest paid in the club's history, opening his account on £12,500 a year. He had carved out a reputation as an uncompromising centre-forward in playing days with Gillingham, Portsmouth, Watford and Charlton.

He had cut his managerial teeth on tough and unglamorous tasks at Yeovil and Oxford United, displaying the sort of unyielding qualities the Canaries felt they needed at this time. A strict disciplinarian, he nailed up the working man's creed immediately on booking in at Carrow Road in the summer of 1969 and promptly began marching his troops up and down the testing slopes of Mousehold on the edge of the city.

Our first face-to-face conversation, him stripped to the waist and flexing muscles and me fiddling with a loose tie and mopping anxious brow, made it clear what sort of relationship he expected: 'I don't want you going on and on about past glories, especially that FA Cup run ten years ago. That's history... I'm here to write a new chapter of success, and I'll do it my way'. A proud boast and stark warning rolled into one.

Sweeping changes didn't end at putting players through a training mangle that wrung out enough sweat to sink the River End. It wasn't long before this no-nonsense boss saw fit to tamper with sacred Canary ideology on the terraces in the name of progress. *On The Ball, City!*, the stirring anthem destined to strike naked fear into opponents and their followers with such spellbinding force during that magical Cup run of 1959, was suddenly dismissed as a bit of a dirge.

I mustered the temerity to suggest to Mr Saunders later in his reign that he hadn't heard it sweep across the pitch with heart-rending fervour simply because his teams and their style never inspired it. I had beat a hasty retreat from his office before that little gem hit home. He despised what he saw as smart-alec

replies or any kind of droll observation at the expense of his
tactics or personnel. He never came to terms with my home-
made Norfolk asides and steadfastly refused to accept 'squit'
had any part to play on the serious soccer scene.

He even complained when I gave familiar clichés my own
treatment, claiming 'The Canaries fluttered to deceive' was
neither clever nor appropriate when an away performance
petered out after a highly promising first 15 minutes.

Ron plotted a deliberate course towards some kind of ogre
figure he deemed necessary to shake up the weak-hearted. At
times that meant the manager resented any kind of outside
judgement on what he was striving to achieve on thin resources.

My genuine efforts to be fair – and I constantly told him I
lived and worked among many die-hard supporters – scarcely
made an impression. Our differences of opinion boiled over
into open warfare after an article criticising one of his key
players, forward Peter Silvester.

'For Pete's sake, goals must come!' ran the headline over
my considered piece in the *Eastern Evening News*. I refused to
apologise after a heated debate on the team bus on the way to
a match – and took the broad hint to disembark at Newmarket.

That left quite a few miles to get to Blackpool, so I caught
a bus to Cambridge, boarded a train going somewhere towards
Lancashire and arrived at the seaside hotel a few minutes before
the official Norwich City party. I waited in the foyer to ask Ron
if they had enjoyed a good journey. I'm still surprised I was fit
enough to take my place in the press box the following day.

We went weeks without discussing club activities in any
depth. I picked up team news by phone, fully aware the
manager was listening in the event of my providing any
well-chosen remarks about his selection. I was banished from
the Carrow Road boardroom after home games for a spell
while general access to players and officials was blocked. Scant

backing from top brass at Prospect House, home of local newspapers just a holler or two from Carrow Road, made me even more determined to write as I saw it.

Any players I did bump into away from the ground were largely sympathetic to my cause. Duncan Forbes, Dave Stringer and Kevin Keelan, at the heart of City's much-employed 'they shall not pass' creed, offered their own brands of affable support, usually coated in 'his bark is worse than his bite' sentiments.

Peter Silvester told me 30 years later, at a happy reunion of the 1972 promotion-winning squad, that he and his wife (pregnant at the time of that notorious article) did not take serious exception to the words which saw me forced to make fresh travel plans to Blackpool. 'We accepted the article as part and parcel of a footballer's lot,' said Peter.

Winger Steve Grapes, one of many to find the Saunders style a bit too painful for comfort, gave me this colourful verdict after a gruelling stint on the training beat: 'He makes bloody Hitler look like Edith Cavell!' It was also claimed this manager made one player feel so inadequate that the poor creature dug a hole in which to hide – and then was told to do extra training because he took too long to dig it.

Dear Ron's impeccable sense of timing and rollicking sense of humour came to the fore with a couple of items on his shopping list. The 1971 Christmas Eve session for overworked but sociable journalists had reached that tantalising 'must be my round' stage when the pub door burst open. It was a chap from our office.

Santa Saunders had bought a player? Pull the other one – it's got jingle bells on!

Eventually, the agitated messenger convinced us that his journey was necessary and I was volunteered to ensure news of Phil Hubbard's £20,000 move from Lincoln made late editions of the *Eastern Evening News* amid a few murmurs about thoughtless soccer managers.

Jim Bone completed the pre-promotion buying programme. With Peter Silvester forced out of the closing stages of the campaign by a cartilage operation, City had a new front man. The £30,000 capture from Partick Thistle filled the gap admirably. The most adventurous Canary since Hugh Curran, Bone did his best to bury the Canaries' image as an efficient but colourless force.

Saunders was in jocular mood when he unveiled his latest signing. Before the jocularity, however, came a prime example of the manager's flair for drama – and I was on the receiving end of a command performance.

It had been a hectic afternoon with calls to Carrow Road every few minutes for a check on latest developments. The story of the player bought to inspire the big promotion push was ready to roll, together with another tribute to the boss who defied economic restrictions. The clock had hurtled round to 3.10, perilously close to deadline, when the all-clear sounded. Just in time.

Down at the ground, though, Saunders emerged with a deep frown and a hand across his furrowed brow. 'Go and scrap the story' he muttered. 'It's all off.' I pointed out that I was very sorry but the edition had gone and would be adorning a few thousand tea tables within the hour.

The worried look across the desk gave way to a cheeky beam. He liked having the original fall-guy around the place now and again. Jim Bone stepped out of the boardroom for a chat.

The newly-arrived Scot made memorable amends for his role in that little charade by providing me with part of the ammunition to fire myself to headline glory when the Canaries won at Charlton on Easter Saturday and moved closer to life in the top flight. He and his fellow striker were on target to inspire 'HOT CROSS BONE DAY' on top of my *Pink Un* match report.

There have been other claims to that tasty line over the years – but I can still call witnesses to prove I had suggested the evening before in a Norwich pub that it would do the job perfectly if David Cross and Jim Bone shared winning goals at The Valley. Not quite in the 'BLY BLY BABES' bracket after City's epic FA Cup victory over Manchester United in 1959 – but one of my better pun-loving moments.

Saunders did mellow a bit when it became clear his parade-ground methods could reap rewards. Even so, he remained suspicious of me in particular and reporters in general. There was more than a dash of 'I told you so!' behind the smile and clenched fist on the night of April 24, 1972, when City won 2-1 at Orient to clinch promotion to Division One for the first time. They made sure of the championship at Watford in the rain the following Saturday with a 1-1 draw.

The end certainly justified the means for the hard man from Birkenhead. Yes, he transformed a club with a Second Division complex into title material inside three seasons. He also paved the way to Wembley for the first time in the club's history with his brand of true grit. He regarded briar patches as inevitable before the chance came to sniff the roses. He believed piles of graft could compensate for limitations in skill. In short, he banked on sweat and dedication rather than the cheque book. I did admire his achievements, particularly as his path to glory was dotted with austerity signs. He stands tall in Norwich City history as a manager who made a lot out of a little.

For all that, he should have accepted an automatic right for sports reporters to honestly reflect their own opinions and the obvious feelings of thousands of spectators at matches when artistry and ambition surrendered all too blatantly to stifling caution. There were plenty of games like that before the promotion sun came out. The 'Gentlemen of the Press' were not the only ones Saunders disliked being critical and asking questions. A long-running feud with City chairman Arthur South came to a head with a scribbled note of resignation in November, 1973, after a 3-1 Carrow Road defeat at the hands of Everton – the club against whom the Canaries started First Division life with a 1-1 draw in August 1972.

Arthur had succeeded Geoffrey Watling as chairman – and playfully chided all reporters as 'Scribes and Pharisees'. He admitted from the start that his relationship with the manager was bound to include occasional 'hard words between two hard men'. A successful businessman and shrewd politician approaching legendary status in Norwich was not likely to flinch from a few bruising rounds with a manager whose sergeant-major tactics had taken Norwich City to a new level… but now needed much more than that to keep them there.

Let me consult my *Eastern Daily Press* notebook to give a flavour of that fateful day when a fraught relationship spilled over into a boardroom explosion:

'For once, the after-match "inquest" deserved such a title. As if sensing a black patch in Carrow Road history, boardroom regulars went into agitated huddles. Knots of reporters paced corridors like sentinels of doom. It was an eerie atmosphere, accentuated by Ron Saunders' appearance with a plate of cakes.

'He smiled and asked if anyone was waiting to see him, supporting claims that his men had scored all Everton's goals. "Duncan Forbes got two and Dave Stringer the other" he said with the dull acceptance of a man ticking off names on an extra-long Christmas shopping list. He moved on to his office – with the cakes.

'Chairman Arthur South had an equally broad smile in the boardroom as he shook hands with Everton directors and manager Billy Bingham. They said they looked forward to seeing him later in the

campaign. He told us he was looking forward to reading Monday's papers and volunteered the suggestion that the City side contained five or six players short of the necessary skills to fight Division One battles.

'As I pointed out this was evident at the start of last season, and the chairman made no attempt to disagree, a Fleet Street reporter whispered 'is his first name Arthur?' and made for a telephone. Even so, there were no strong hints at this stage of the angry confrontation to come – and the end of Ron Saunders' reign as Norwich City manager.'

I had sensed strongly a couple of weeks before that a top-level rift was in danger of becoming a hopeless split. Clear indications that the relationship wasn't just strained but cracking open were given when the Canaries flew to Merseyside for their League Cup tie with Everton. (Note how the Toffees keep sticking to this troublesome saga). The tradition of chairman and manager sitting together was not observed.

This was one of the rare occasions in that era when reporters travelled with the team – Saunders put paid to that arrangement about two years earlier – and it would have been naïve to overlook furtive whispers and knowing nods that greeted a 'separate ways' policy.

I understood Saunders had been given some kind of ultimatum about buying players shortly before collecting £150,000 for the sale of David Cross to Coventry. Undoubtedly the manager had complained constantly about a shortage of ready cash. I wrote a few weeks before he was likely to sell one or two of his established players before taking much-needed plunges into the transfer market.

After that article in the *Eastern Daily Press*, Mr South told me at Norwich Airport, when the flight to Merseyside was held up by fog, that I had miscalculated on certain points. The real trouble, he claimed, was that the manager was not bringing possible signings to them. Money wasn't the beginning and end of it all.

Obviously, patience was wearing thin on the board as the

Canaries carried an ominous struggling look after walking the relegation tightrope the season before. However, while lack of action on the transfer front was the main bone of contention as crunch day approached, there were other contributory factors. Saunders felt on at least two occasions the chairman had left him out in the cold.

Arthur's 'attacking football' pledge on succeeding Geoffrey Watling was not greeted kindly by a feisty manager who considered it his job to formulate playing policy. Then players found 'Clean up your game' letters in their pay packets. The chairman, thought to have put them there, told me it was a personal matter between board and players. No reference to the manager.

Shortly after Saunders' dramatic departure, with recriminations still thick in the air, the Norwich chairman took the most unusual step of showing me minutes of board meetings at which the manager was strongly urged to bring potential signings to the table.

Perhaps it was reference to those revelations in one of my columns soon after that led to another dose of the old Saunders medicine at Villa Park just before Christmas, 1975. Now in charge of Aston Villa, he banned me from the post-match conference when the Canaries paid a visit. He didn't like some of the things I'd written on his departure from Norfolk.

'You didn't go a lot on some of the things I wrote while you were there!' I offered as a parting shot.

My young colleague, a promising lad on the *Eastern Evening News*, added, 'If he's not good enough to talk to, nor am I'. I was truly uplifted by such a show of solidarity from Mick Dennis as he followed me out of a scowling Saunders' presence.

To show I am not prone to creeping tendencies towards someone who moved on to 'bigger things' in the football reporting world, let me praise the two other colleagues who kept me cheerfully positive throughout truly challenging seasons. They persuaded me more than once apiece not to pack it all in and try my luck at becoming Norfolk's soul sensation as Skip with the Sugar Beets.

Bruce Robinson, the sound philosopher to my youthful extrovert, the well-organised essayist to my rather racy, pun-loving contributor, regularly exploited my lamentable defensive play at comb and penny football played on train compartment tables. Bruce died, aged 80, in June 2016.

Chris Erskine would break into Pompey Chimes at the most inappropriate times – like in a silent press box at Southampton – and reduced me to helpless laughter on Merseyside the night before an Anfield fixture by informing anyone who'd listen, 'My ears are cold!'

When the Bondwagon started rolling, and Carrow Road became a more colourful and welcoming place, the Canaries soon unpeeled that well-stuck label for being boring travellers. Such a contrast in styles after the safety-first Saunders era, not least towards an ever-hungry publicity machine, often caused me to wonder if this was the same club pursuing the same goals in the same sport.

One Fleet Street veteran, who had seen more soccer managers come and go than I'd eaten late breakfasts, suggested a few months into Bond's reign that drastic surgery could be the answer. 'If you could melt down the two managers and mix the steel and organisation of one with the flair and flamboyance of the other, reckon that'd produce just about the perfect boss.'

Bond often needed protection from his non-stop passion to oblige. Cynical operators chasing juicy headlines for the national tabloids made him a regular target. I lost count of the number of times he dived head first into water hot enough to attract the attention of top FA officials.

I devised a weekend format designed to restore a measure of calm and balance to a scene dominated by constant doses of

Saturday tea time fever. With the dust settled and main agitators returned to the capital, I then asked Mr Bond for his more considered opinions on a quiet Sunday afternoon.

This might spell a much more reasoned digest for local Monday morning readers, but such a pragmatic approach back-fired now and then as my editorial lords and masters seriously questioned decisions to ignore the manufactured nonsense decorating Sunday's national back pages!

Perhaps the clearest example of Norwich's ever-helpful boss being set up for a fall came on the eve of the 1975 League Cup final at Wembley against Aston Villa, managed by none other than Ron 'actions-speak-louder than words' Saunders.

Two seasons before, he had taken the Canaries to their first Wembley appearance in the same competition. They had lost by the only goal to Spurs (Ralph Coates) and were widely dismissed as country bores better suited to a gruelling relegation struggle. A beaming Bond was easily persuaded by a notorious tabloid teaser to pledge it wouldn't happen again. The Norwich side would throw caution to the wind and show grumpy old Ron that adventure brings its own reward.

Grumpy's Villa won by the only goal (Ray Graydon) in another instantly forgettable showpiece.

For me, the highlight of the day came later with the sight of a white-suited John Bond strutting down the team hotel's stairs like a nimble-footed John Wayne to rouse deflated troops and deflect them towards Talk of the Town for an audience with his favourite singer, Lena Martell. He could turn on the style – and it counted most when human frailties were cruelly exposed – but I felt there was not enough consistency or order in his managerial style.

Bond's faithful henchman, the ever-smiling Ken Brown, was a perfect foil during their Carrow Road years together. He mended fences his impulsive sidekick trampled down, consoled and then rebuilt the confidence of a player pilloried in public, explained carefully to a waiting reporter what had really been meant by that comment about 'barmy pensioners who run the game' and generally picked up all the litter of discontent and rumour strewn around the place.

That was all useful training for the day he took over as his old friend outgrew the Norfolk stage. Ken was the ideal No.2. The fact he survived seven years as No.1 – and led Norwich to an overdue Wembley success in 1985 – revealed plenty of qualities to go with that easy-going manner and infectious brand of humour. His successor, Dave Stringer, also under-lined the way a 'nice guy' had a perfect right to succeed.

John Bond enjoyed a mainly happy relationship with chair-man Sir Arthur South, knighted in 1974, and other directors although there was plenty of political intrigue going on in the boardroom. This erupted into the open in April, 1976, when Sir Arthur and previous chairman Geoffrey Watling, another hard-headed Carrow Road stalwart who liked his own way, became embroiled in violent verbal exchanges in front of me and other local newspaper colleagues.

It was a complex affair, with Sir Arthur's private life trawled out for public inspection by national tabloid tormentors, but he survived to carry on trying to make some sense of an increasingly volatile business. I prepared to take my leave of full-time football reporting amid growing suspicions our professional game might soon fall foul of ludicrous transfer fees and wages along with cheap celebrity standards and rampant commercialism.

I'm glad I kept going long enough to see a smile or three break out at Carrow Road after what had been a workmanlike grind towards the top flight with few patches of genuine excitement. Colleague Bruce Robinson, who had found his sanctuary from soccer storms in gentler literary waters, said

he'd always considered me rather ill at ease with a game I
wanted to be free-wheeling entertainment rather than a
money-loaded business. I continued to keep a close eye on
Carrow Road affairs and even resumed some regular links as
a match summariser alongside commentator Roy Waller when
BBC Radio Norfolk arrived in 1980. That role reached its
summit in the Milk Cup Final of 1985 when the Canaries at last
provided something to savour at Wembley with a lone-goal win
over Sunderland.

John Bond chipped in with a few of his typically over-
stated observations. I bowed out, my journey from home
village touchline scribe to national stadium success completed.

Norwich City played too big and important a part in my
life so far to leave this slice of the club's history without some
humour, laughter and sporting companionship of enduring
quality. I place Duncan Forbes top of the bill without
hesitation.

His supply of jokes, most of them aired at the expense of
good chum Dave Stringer, never wore thin through constant
repetition simply because of the shameless relish with which he
told them. He loved the one about 'more bookings than Fred
Pontin' because it gave him the chance to emphasise yet again
he was never sent off in his Canary career.

One of his favourite ploys on away trips was to convince
people they had met before, picking up the conversation from
where they'd left off. I was amazed how many times it worked
as he inquired, 'So, how is the lad getting on at university?' or
'And does she still help out with meals-on-wheels?' Several of
his colleagues were impressed at the number of friends he had
made around the country. Unlike most football 'humour', it was
quirky, often funny and totally without malice.

Trevor Hockey arrived from Sheffield United with his long
hair, headband and piratical beard – 'a Blade without a razor'

I called him – to stiffen Canary resolve to beat relegation at the end of the 1972-73 campaign. His buccaneering swagger in midfield was matched by a penchant for plundering as many chuckles as possible from japes on unsuspecting colleagues.

His greatest triumph featured another newcomer to the club who received an urgent call from reception while the team were staying at a Midlands hotel. While he was away attempting to follow the babble of a Canary pretending to be an insurance agent on the phone, Hockey's Furniture Removals sprang into action with a drastic rearranging programme. On his return our hapless victim could only assume he was in the wrong room... and wandered off in search of his rightful quarters. Titters grew into guffaws and then descended into raucous laughter as he approached reception to check the number of his room.

Perhaps my final anecdote is wrapped up more in pathos than laughter – but it stands as a symbol of the defiance with which I tried to counter the unyielding attitude of Hard Man Saunders.

After a lively exchange of opinions on a bitterly cold morning, a shirt-sleeved manager mocked the hunched reporter, streaming with cold over an electric fire in the corner of the office. 'Here you are, you snivelling wretch – a cup of tea with something in it. Probably kill you.' I took it, sipped and looked him straight in the eye. I mustered every ounce of Norfolk cussedness in my ailing body and announced: 'I'll be about here long after you've gone, ole partner!'

I could have sworn he nearly smiled.

Keith Skipper reported on Norwich City for the *Eastern Daily Press* and for Radio Norfolk before becoming an author, broadcaster and entertainer who has championed his native Norfolk in books and on DVDs. He founded Friends Of Norfolk Dialect to archive the county's traditional words, became Deputy Lieutenant for Norfolk in 2003 and was made an MBE in 2007 for services to the community.

3

The chant used to be, 'Ru-el! Ru-el!' It
echoed around grounds as Norwich
fans saluted **Ruel Fox**. But he tells us
here about the racism that greeted him
when he joined the club as a schoolboy.

His is a story of glory, though – of
how he went on to play a leading role
as the team roared up the Premier
League and then launched a
barnstorming European campaign.

FROM ABUSE TO BEATING BAYERN

BY RUEL FOX

I grew up in Ipswich, but it was how Norwich reacted when I had trials with them that made me choose them.

I learned my skills playing in a park in games with about 20 on each team, and by playing kerbsy on the Whitton estate, where I lived with my mum, three brothers and a sister. I did have trials at Ipswich, and they asked me to go back the next week, but I had trials at Norwich arranged and went there instead. I had three sessions at Norwich and Ken Brown, who was manager at Carrow Road, phoned my mum and said, 'We want him.'

He appointed Ronnie Brooks, who had been a scout and now worked with the youth team, to be a sort of minder for me. They said they would give one of my brothers, Lennie, petrol money to drive me up the A140, because I was only 15. They sorted me out with kit and stuff, because my mum couldn't afford to buy it all.

It wasn't that I didn't want to play for Ipswich. It was about the opportunity that I was offered at Norwich, the way they made it clear that they wanted me, and my gut feeling, which was that, at the time, Norwich were a little bit ahead in football terms.

But I can't lie about what happened, and I have to say the first time I encountered racism to any great extent was when I started playing for Norwich, and some of it came from lads in my team.

Ipswich was a safe place in terms of racism. There were a lot of people from Afro-Caribbean backgrounds. On my estate alone it was probably 30 per cent black people and our school team had about five black lads in it. I knew about racism, of course, but never came across it really. Then I got to Norwich and I was the only black player in the team.

Norwich had devised this scheme for a team that was a mix between youth players who weren't getting a game on the Saturday, trialists and schoolboys they had signed. The team played in a men's Sunday league. It was full of hung-over pub-team players, and the last thing they wanted was some nippy youngsters scooting around them. So they would often try and stop us with fouls. I can kind of understand that and it was a growing up process for me.

I started to hear quite a lot of little snidey things like, 'Pick up the blackie' and that sort of thing. There wasn't too much of the n-word but it wasn't right. Ronnie Brooks, who was there for me at every match, would get involved if he heard anything and my brother Lennie was often having a go back at someone while the game was going on.

Just before I signed as an apprentice, Norwich asked me to go on a youth team tour because I was doing so well for the Sunday team. I didn't have a passport, so my mum had to rush about and get me one organised. I was really excited, but when I joined the tour group, Dale Gordon and me were the only non-white players. No disrespect to Dale, but he is from an Indian background and is light-skinned.

There were little, nasty comments from some of the youth players towards me about me being black. I went to Ronnie and told him. He went to the players and sorted it out. And Mark Farrington, who was in the team as an over-age player, confronted some of them about it for me.

So there were people dealing with it. If Ken Brown ever

heard about any of the stuff that went on, he would always crack down on it. I could stick up for myself as well, though, and fronted some of them out about it. There is no excuse for that sort of thing. It used to upset me when Norwich fans said racist stuff to opponents. I'd look at them and they'd sort of go, 'Not you Foxy', as if that made it all right.

As a youngster, to get it from boys who were meant to be on your own side in a match was certainly not nice, but as soon as I started to get further along with my career, the same ones were on the phone to me asking me to get them tickets. Some of them are on my Facebook page now and they must know that I remember what they were like.

It was things like switching the light off in the room at night and saying, 'Who's the odd one out?' and that sort of thing. But I have never confronted them on Facebook and said, 'I remember what you were like when I was a schoolboy'.

My story speaks for itself, though. I progressed so quickly that I wasn't around these players for long and before I knew it, I was in the first team at 17 and some of these lads were now my apprentices, cleaning my boots.

I don't forget the stuff that went on, even now. It is part of who I am and what I had to overcome. Just as part of it was growing up as the youngest of five children with a single-parent mum who had it quite tough.

Over the road from my mum's place was where Louie Donowa had grown up. He was nearly four years older than me and was in the Norwich team who won the Milk Cup in 1985. When he was first getting into the team, I was 14 and would see him come home in a nice, new car and listen to him saying how great it was at Norwich. He was good to me and gave me a pair of his boots. I started pestering him to get me a trial at Norwich and he did. He set up the trial that led to Ken Brown telling my mum, 'We want him'.

I was fast-tracked at Norwich and my first involvement with the first team came when Ken Brown took me on a trip to an away game as experience. On the way back, the lads were all encouraging me to have a few beers, and I had a few too many. I was bladdered and went into the toilet on the bus to be sick. Someone locked me in there and they all left me there for the rest of the trip. Back in Norwich the driver discovered me and let me out, but everyone else had long gone. That was my initiation.

Of course, of my time at Norwich, two seasons stand out: 1992-93, when we finished third in the first ever Premier League season, and 1993-94 when we played in the club's first European campaign.

Over those two seasons a lot of players took part, but the regulars over both seasons were Bryan Gunn in goal, Ian Culverhouse and Mark Bowen at full back, Ian Crook in midfield and Chris Sutton in attack. I was the first choice at right midfield, and then there were players like Jerry Goss, Rob Newman, John Polston, Ian Butterworth, Gary Megson, Mark Robbins and Efan Ekoku.

Efan was fast. I wasn't too slow either, but in a race between me and him, he would definitely win. I was quick over a short distance, but he was blistering, and he had those long legs so I'd have had no chance in a race with him.

Darren Eadie was another who was quick and he got into the team during the European run, so we had a really pacy team.

'Chippy' Crook was the most underrated midfield player who was around at that time and for me, having Chippy in the team meant that I just developed all the time. He and the others who came from Tottenham – Bowen, Culverhouse and Polston – were at such a level when they arrived that you benefitted from what they did and you learned too.

At Norwich I always played out wide. I think because Louie

Donowa had been a success in that position, as soon as I went for my trial at Norwich they put me there too. For the first few years at the club, I used to just go past people on the outside. When I started to get a run in the first team I did a lot more work on going inside as well and using my left foot for more than standing on. It was only under Mike Walker that I had a consistent run in the first team and then it became apparent to people how I was beating opponents, so defenders would try to send me inside. I had to work on being effective that way as well, and I took it on myself to start practising, practising and practising.

I enjoyed getting the better of a full back. Why wouldn't I? And if I could set something up then for a team-mate, well that was job done. Lots of the chances I set up were for Chris Sutton – which is what I tell him if I see him now.

It was sometimes a sharp ball in towards the near post so that he could get across in front of his defender and get a touch. Sometimes it was a far post ball for him to attack. It was a mixture. You sometimes find a player that you click with and Chris and me did that straight from the start.

At first Norwich couldn't make their mind up with Chris whether he was a striker or a centre-half. But all of a sudden he got a few goals and it was obvious he had to be a striker. Once Mike Walker took over and I got in the team regularly, my understanding with Chris just happened. I knew everything he wanted to do almost before he did and we were just in sync. So every time I got the ball, I knew where he was and where he would go. It became instinctive.

We also went out socially and hung out with each other, and with Lee Power. We were from different backgrounds but we hung about all day together. The other players used to call us the Bostick Brothers, because we stuck together. After train-ing we would go down Riverside and have a drink and something to eat and then find something to do: snooker, or arcade machines or something, but whatever it was, we'd all go and do it. It was like being back at school with your mates and I loved it. I stayed at Chris's parents' house sometimes, and they looked after me brilliantly.

It wasn't a clique so that when we got to training we didn't speak to anyone else. It wasn't like that at all. We just had a laugh, and when Tim Sherwood came to the club, he was another who liked to be joking and so we had a group of players who just really enjoyed being with each other.

For that first season of the new Premier League, 1992-93, there was no sudden change in the way we played. There were certainly no restrictions placed on us: it wasn't a case of the manager pulling us in and saying, 'Look, don't do this or that during a game.'

The situation with Mike Walker was a strange one. We talk about coaches finding it hard to be a manager but I don't think he found it hard at all, because I don't think he really needed to manage us. We knew him as the reserves' manager, and someone who would muck about and have a laugh. Then, when he became first team manager, he didn't really change. Of course there were disagreements over the course of the season but the majority of the time he was like one of the lads. It was quite refreshing, and we responded by playing some great stuff, perhaps because we were relaxed.

John Deehan did the first team coaching and that was brilliant for me and Chris because he had been a great striker and was happy to give up time to have extra sessions with us.

Playing for Norwich, every away game is a long trip, and on the bus you'd have a card school at the back. Lee Power loved his cards. But I never really got involved. I just sat nearer the front and played arcade games on my Atari.

I'm being honest in this book so I have to say the game definitely had a drinking culture. This was a time before dieticians and the like at football clubs, of course. I always roomed with Chris and that season when we finished third in the Premier League, I can't remember us having an early night.

I am not talking about going out or having loads of women back or anything like that. I am talking about just sitting up in the hotel room and perhaps sneaking a bottle of red and sitting around talking. There was none of this stuff that goes on now at some clubs, with the assistant manager or someone patrolling the corridor. And there was certainly no Mike Walker checking up on us, because he was often still downstairs having a drink as well.

I know that one night before a game in the 1993-94 season we didn't get to bed until after 3am. Somebody smuggled a crate of beer in there and we had computer games.

The next day we were at Leeds and we weren't expected to get anything, so we were very relaxed, just went out and played, and we won 4-0. I got two, Chris got one and Jerry Goss got one of his screamers.

We had a relaxed manager with a relaxed regime and yet we had the best two seasons the club has ever had before or since. I think it was a combination of things, but we definitely had good players who all peaked at the same time. Players do have a peak, and most of us hit our purple patches at the same time. There was no magic potion or clever tactics: just good players, at their peak, encouraged to play.

John Deehan would talk about the opposition, their strengths and weaknesses and how they would play, but we were never restricted because of what he told us. Mike would allow me to go where I wanted on the pitch, as long as we all filled in for each other. So, instead of staying out wide on the right, which is what most wingers would do, I began to copy what I had seen Ryan Giggs do, which was to swap wings from time to time, or have a run up the middle. That made it a nightmare for a team who had set up with a full back to mark me because suddenly I was coming through the middle and joining in with the strikers, and the full back is just watching from his position out wide.

We were definitely close to being champions in 1992-93. We started by winning at Arsenal, which nobody expected, and after that we thought we could take on anyone.

I used to get on with people like Ian Wright, so there was a bit of banter in the tunnel before the game against Arsenal at Highbury. And I really used to enjoy playing against Nigel Winterburn, who was supposed to mark me. I always liked the challenge of trying to get the better of him. We were 2-0 down at half-time but got four in the second half. I got the last goal.

We won seven of our first nine games, only losing once. That included beating Chelsea home and away. It was a phe-nomenal run, but we got smashed 7-1 at Blackburn and 4-1 at Liverpool and we still had a negative goal difference when we got to the top of the table before Christmas.

I remember we had a tough game at Oldham at the start of November, where we just edged to a 3-2 win, and then we went on a run of three more wins that included a victory at Aston Villa, who were right near the top of the table. We thought they were probably the best team, better even than Manchester United, and when we beat Villa on their own ground, it was a really big win.

But, after beating Wimbledon at Carrow Road before Christmas, we went six games without a win.

Then, in the run-in, we beat Villa again at Carrow Road to keep ourselves in with a chance but in the next home game we got torn apart by United, which set them up to win the title and left us having to settle, eventually, for third, with Villa second.

It was the closest Norwich City had ever been to being champions and you have to think it might be the closest the club will ever get. We loved it when we were top. The chairman, Robert Chase, let us fly to away games, and we just loved it all. We certainly liked the win bonuses. But we weren't ever thinking, 'What if we actually win the league?' People might think we didn't take it seriously enough but I honestly think if we had taken it a lot more seriously we would not have got the results we did.

We couldn't see the future, of course. We didn't know how the Premier League would develop, with clubs like United leaving clubs like Norwich a long, long way behind financially. It wasn't a shock to the country that Norwich finished third – nothing like the outrageous shock of Leicester winning the title in 2015-16 was.

And so when we came back for the start of the next season, we just kept doing what we'd been doing. The difference was that we had European matches to look forward to, though.

Our bonuses were more than the wages for some players, so we were more worried that the chairman was going to pay them on time than thinking seriously about winning the UEFA Cup. We were just like, 'Let's see how far we can go.'

Winning at Bayern Munich was special, though, of course. Until another Norwich team achieves something like it, that night will stand out as the single high-point for the club, I would say.

I remember the pitch was big and seemed even bigger because there was a running track around the outside, so that the crowd was a long way away from us. But although that game has become a piece of history, we just went out and played again. We'd been happy to get past Vitesse Arnhem in the first round and didn't feel under any pressure in Munich, so we played with the freedom that allowed Gossy to volley that famous goal and allowed Marky Bowen, a full back, to get into their box for our second goal.

Winning was a dream. The first thing we were thinking was, 'Whose top can I swap with?' It was the same when we drew the second leg at Carrow Road to beat them on aggregate. I got the Brazilian Jorginho's shirt after the home leg and there's a picture of me that I've seen where I am celebrating in the Bayern shirt at the end of the game. I've still got that shirt, framed.

The Germans didn't like losing to us. They didn't handle it very well. There wasn't any handshakes or any of them saying, 'Well done'. They just got themselves off the pitch. We weren't worried about that though, and we had a great night out in the city celebrating with supporters. We knew the DJ at Ritzy's on Tombland and he would get us in to the VIP area there. But we didn't stay there long because there were lots of other bars and clubs to go to.

The mood was brilliant after the Bayern game, but we often went out and mixed with the fans. I don't remember too many incidents where anyone gave us any grief. It was just how it was then, that Norwich players could go out in the city and have a drink with fans. And of course, we were getting good results so everyone liked us anyway. We knew a place where the players would get free pizza, and another place where we got free Chinese meals so we always went on the same route around the different places.

After Bayern, we were drawn against Internazionale in the next round. Perhaps Bayern had underestimated us, but Inter were on guard against an upset and, from the kick-off, you could tell they were on a different level in terms of fitness and sharpness. They had Dennis Bergkamp and Ruben Sosa in attack, too.

The first leg was at Carrow Road. They had a man on me all game, and they closed us down very effectively. Then, after about an hour of the first game, they went up another gear. We didn't concede until ten minutes from the end, when Rob

Newman couldn't quite catch Bergkamp legally and gave away a penalty.

For the second leg, we had injuries and suspensions and lost 1-0 again. We'd gone as far as we could.

But because of our success over a season and a half, there was speculation that other clubs would be after some of the high-profile players. So there was pressure on the club to give us new contracts with better wages and I had several meetings with them saying, 'Well, what are we going to do now?'

The truth is that I could feel that the period when all the players were at their peaks wasn't going to last too much longer. Unless the club started refreshing the squad, I was worried that we would be two-season wonders.

Then, out of the blue, Mike Walker went to Everton. It was only a month after we'd finished our UEFA Cup run and I couldn't believe it. He was a good coach and a good motivator but to manage our group hadn't been difficult for him and yet now he was going to Everton with their history, expectations and lots more pressure.

'Dixie' Deehan took over and we were happy with that because it was not a massive upheaval. But about a month after Mike went, I got a call from the chairman as I was driving in to training and he asked me to go straight to his office. I did and he told me Newcastle had made an offer and he was close to agreeing a fee. I didn't know what to say to that and so I actually asked, 'What do you want me to say?'

He said, 'I am telling you that you can go up there and speak to Kevin Keegan. There is no point in me saying I will offer you a better contract to stay because you are already on our top wages so I can't bluff you. But if you go and speak to him and it doesn't work out for you, nobody will know and you can just come back here'.

I'd only played for Norwich and didn't know what the

procedure was with transfers, so when I left the office I drove home instead of to training and talked to my wife. I thought there can't be any harm flying to Newcastle just to speak to them. In my head, that was all I was doing because that is what the chairman had told me.

By the time I had driven from my home to Stansted Airport, the chairman had apparently told the press that I had turned down a new contract and was going to join Newcastle. So, with that, I decided I wasn't coming back. I was adamant. I felt I had been put in a position that was wrong.

It was a shame that was how my days at Norwich ended, but for my football career, Newcastle seemed right. I got there and was greeted by two of the biggest legends of the game, Kevin Keegan, who was the Newcastle manager, and Terry McDermott, his assistant. They had played together for Liverpool and Newcastle, and when I was growing up they were the sort of player I dreamed of becoming.

They talked to me for an hour and that was that. Then they put me up in a hotel, and I didn't even go back home to get any stuff or see my wife. They said they would fly her up and sort out all the stuff. That was how much they wanted me and that was the contrast with what had just happened at Norwich.

Keegan spoke to me about racism, but in a positive way. He said, 'There are a lot of National Front up here. But if you do well here, you will change their perspective.' So he set me a challenge, and that was a masterstroke.

Andy Cole had only been there a short while. He was the only black player in their team and he'd had some problems regarding racism, but my arrival helped him. That was another clever piece of thinking by Kevin.

It was February 1994. I went straight into the Newcastle team, we finished third and qualified for the UEFA Cup, which was history repeating itself for me. This isn't the place to talk about Newcastle, though, or about my time at Tottenham, which came next.

But I will say that it was while I was at Tottenham that my wife and I bought a house in Colchester, and that is where I still live.

For a while I was chairman of Whitton Town FC, the club near where I grew up, on the outskirts of Ipswich. I have always had a connection with them. When I was at Norwich I would often go to Whitton's ground after I'd played a game. I took over as chairman because they needed someone, but it was always going to be temporary.

I still spend time at Whitton, though. It's where I deliver sessions for my business now, which is a fitness boot camp. I love it, because it is something I understand after all the years of training to perform as a footballer, and because I can change lives.

Despite my Norwich past, Ipswich fans are okay with me – until we play them! No, they're all right, probably because I grew up in the area and know so many people in the town.

Despite how it ended, I am not negative at all about my time at Norwich. It was the best education I could have had. They gave me Ronnie Brooks and they looked after me. I couldn't have had a better start anywhere. They were the club who gave me the opportunity to play football. They encouraged and helped me and I developed because, at Norwich, I played alongside some top, top players.

Ruel Fox joined Norwich as a schoolboy and was a pro at the club from 1986 to 1994. He was a leading member of perhaps the best-ever City side, who finished third in the Premier League and then, the next season, had an historic European campaign. His dashing style made him a favourite with supporters, whose vote made him an inaugural member of the club's Hall of Fame. After Norwich he played for Newcastle and Tottenham.

4

Dave Stringer is 'one of our own'. He has lived all his life in Norfolk – and gave all but four years of his entire playing, coaching and management career to Norwich City.

His tale is an honest account about himself and the club he still calls his own. In a matter-of-fact tone that says much about him, he recaps achievements that were anything but modest.

So here, for the first time and in his own words, is the full story of a man who was one of the foundation blocks on which the modern-day club was built.

IT MATTERED BECAUSE I CARED

BY DAVE STRINGER

My father negotiated my first professional contract with Norwich City and got me a very good deal: £15 a week basic, £7 10s (£7.50 now) for every first team appearance, £4 for a win and £2 for a draw. If the team got in the top eight in our division, and if I played sufficient games, there was £750 at stake – but that was to be shared among the whole team!

Before my father intervened, I'd been ready to snap their hand off for the £12 a week they were offering, because I just wanted to play football for my local professional club.

I was 18. I'd left Alderman Leach School in Gorleston at 15 and started an apprenticeship in engineering. Football was what I wanted to do, though.

I used to go and watch Yarmouth Town, who played at the Wellesley, like they do now. They were in the Eastern Counties League and they used to play the 'A' teams of clubs like Chelsea and West Ham.

At Alderman Leach with me were Peter Simpson, who went on to play for Arsenal, and Mike Bailey, who played for Wolves. Peter and I actually had a trial for Arsenal at the same time, because we played for the county together and both got invited down to London. Peter got taken on and I didn't.

But I was in the Gorleston first team at 16, and then started playing for Norwich City 'B' team. But it was only when I was picked for the England Youth team, that Ron Ashman, who was the Norwich manager at the time, decided to offer me professional terms – and my father struck that hard bargain on my behalf.

This was 1963, and if I'd stayed in engineering and become fully qualified, I'd have probably been on £12 a week. So professional football was good money, but not out of sight of working men.

I'd been a centre forward in schools football, scoring lots of goals. But Gorleston made me a full back, and that is what I was when I became a pro at Norwich. There was a lot to learn as a young player, and I didn't get into the first team until near the end of the 1964-65 season, when I was 20. Norwich were in the second tier – they had never been any higher than that – and Ashman gave two or three of us our debuts in a game at Coventry, but we lost 3-0 and it was a bit or a rude awakening for me.

I was excited, of course, and wanting to show I was capable of playing at that level. But as a young player in a big match for the first time, you sometimes take more notice of the occasion than the game. So I can remember the atmosphere, the crowd and so on, but the game went past in a flash. As I got more experience, I learned to concentrate solely on the game, and it didn't matter how many people were there or anything other than the game itself.

I played three matches in the remainder of that season, but wasn't picked at the start of the following season. You have to remember that there were no substitutes then, so you were either in the team or not a part of it at all.

Then Phil Kelly, a Republic of Ireland full back who was in the team at that time, suffered a bad knee injury: cruciate ligaments, which was a career-ending injury then. Freddie Sharpe, who was ex-Tottenham, got into the team but didn't do too well, so for the game against Cardiff, I was given a chance. I grabbed it, and from then on, my aim was to play well enough to keep in the team. There were some good players in that side: people like Ron Davies, Terry Bly, Mal Lucas, Gordon Bolland, and in goal was a twenty-something called Kevin Keelan.

It was a good side, but the club had never really looked like getting into the top division. Ashman left, Lol Morgan came in, but the highest we finished in that period was ninth.

To tell you the truth, I was getting itchy feet a little bit, because I wanted to play at the top level. I had the ambition to play at the highest level I could but it seemed as if I was running out of time to do that and that the club was just plodding along.

It was when Ron Saunders came, at the start of the 1969-70 season, that the club changed, and so did my career and life. My attitude didn't change, but Ron's attitude matched mine.

He was what the club needed at that time: someone to pull it up by the bootstraps. He did exactly that. He was a no-nonsense man who didn't mess about at all. Either you did it his way or you were out.

For the first pre-season, he was in shorts and stripped to the waist and he looked the part: fit and strong. He sat on the ball in the middle of the group and he said, 'Right. I want to get this team into the First Division. Those who don't want to come with me, I'll see in my office after training'.

So we thought, 'There's going to be no messing with this one'. And I thought, 'You'll do me'. I thought he was someone I could look up to and respect.

His face had a jutting chin and he looked like he was carved from granite. And when he played in some of the games in training, he was a tough man.

He drilled and drilled and drilled the team in the way he wanted us to play. We were so fit that we ran teams off the park. They couldn't stay with us. We got the ball forward quickly and the back line got up field as fast as we could, so of course the opposition forwards had to come with us. In fact they did more running trying to catch us up to keep onside. We made them work hard. So when the ball was coming back the other way, they just didn't have the energy to go forward.

To get us that fit, the training was really fierce. Pre-season, the amount of work was amazing. For example we would prob-ably do 100 exercises on our legs only, going around the outside of the pitch. We would jump over sticks while carrying weights, and that sort of thing.

The fashion then was for flared trousers, but Stephen Grapes, a young winger some of you will remember, couldn't even find a pair of flares that would go over his thighs because they blew up so that they were like tree-trunks because of all the work Ron made him and the rest of us do.

I have never felt so fit in all my playing career. We did have some players with skill and craft, men like Dougie Livermore, Kenny Foggo, Jimmy Bone and David Cross, but our play was based on our fitness and those sort of players had to work hard as well.

I had moved to centre back under Lol Morgan. And it was Lol who bought Duncan Forbes. We didn't play similarly, Duncan and me. Our personalities were very different, too. But the similarity between us was that we didn't want to lose – at anything we did. If you played table tennis against Duncan it would go on for ever. He would just keep getting the ball back and wait for you to make mistakes. He was so hard to play against, and he was like that as a footballer.

Forwards playing against him just thought, 'Oh for good-ness' sake, give me a rest.'

He was strong in the opposing penalty area as well, and we both scored goals. He would say himself that he wasn't blessed with the greatest of skills but he stopped those who were skilled playing and he was very effective. When he became captain, he was effective at that too, because he was a natural leader.

This was the era of 4-4-2, so every team had two up-front. Virtually every team played like that and Duncan and I would pick up the two strikers. Normally the opposition had a little and large situation: a big, strong striker, and a small, nippy striker playing off him. Duncan always liked to pick up the big feller who would be working down the middle and who was going to be fighting for the ball. So I would then have to mark the player running off the big centre-forward. I had to do my job when the ball came through the air, too. I had a fairly good leap although I was 5ft 10, which was not big for a centre back. I was happy playing on the right or the left of Duncan, depending on where my man was going.

When Ron Saunders came, he said it would take him three years to get promotion, and he was right. The first year was sorting out what he had, and getting players in. The second year was drilling us into a side, and the third year was to go for promotion. And that is what happened.

A testimony really to the way he did things was that, years later, we all met up again for a testimonial. The 1972 promotion team all played together again and it was like a jigsaw. We all fitted in. We all knew each other's game, still. We knew each other's deficiencies but we knew each other's strengths as well. It was remarkable.

We won promotion at Orient on the Monday night and went to Watford on the Saturday needing a draw for the title ahead of Birmingham. We drew 1-1 and I got the goal – although I should have had three. Kenny Foggo kept putting the ball into the same place and I kept getting my head to it, but two didn't go in. The third one did, though and the film is still available to see, on YouTube.

Millwall, who had run us close all the way through, missed out on promotion, but the top three teams didn't lose at home in the league all season, which shows you it was tight.

I'd had eight seasons in the second tier. I'd begun to fear that I wouldn't get a chance in the top tier. But now, Norwich City were going up into the top division for the very first time, and my goal won the title, which finished off a special season for me.

The following season we got to the League Cup final – the club's first appearance at Wembley – but I think that took something away from our performances in the top tier.

The match that sticks in my mind in the run to Wembley was the Chelsea semi-final. We went to Chelsea and beat them 2-0, which surprised a lot of people, and then, for the second leg at Carrow Road, the ground was packed.

It was a terrific stadium for night games. There were terraces on three sides in those days, and there were 35,000 people plus there. When we walked out that night, the excitement the supporters had – the chance of going to Wembley for the first time – was palpable. You could feel it. The air was electric and, as a player, you couldn't fail to be excited. I had played 400 games or so by then and so I wasn't nervous, but I was definitely excited.

It is hard to describe the feeling. I looked forward to games like that. I wanted to be out there, play and do well. And the ultimate enjoyment would be if we worked hard and won the game.

We were leading 3-2 on the night and 5-2 on aggregate. Terry Anderson, David Cross and Paul Cheesley scored our goals, and we thought we were on our way to Wembley. But then this blanket of fog rolled in from the River End and it did get really bad, so the ref, Gordon Hill, took us all off five minutes from the end.

He told us he was going to see if the fog would lift enough for us to finish the match and I said to Chelsea's David Webb,

'He can't call it off now. We've almost finished. Surely we can play the last few minutes.' Webby said, 'Don't say that. There'll be another bonus for another game.'

We were off the pitch for 17 minutes and the Chelsea fans were singing, 'Come on the fog!' Then the ref took us back out, but after only two more minutes he gave up and abandoned the match.

It was a nerve-wracking wait for the game to be restaged, because I thought the situation had given Chelsea another chance. They would be used to us, and our style, and they would get another crack. But when the game was replayed, we won 1-0.

Playing at Wembley that first time was a terrific experience. There were two months between the semi-final and the final, and all that time there was the build-up in the media. Then playing at Wembley, which was every player's dream, was really special. The manager led the team out, then came Duncan, then Kevin, the goalkeeper, and I was third in the line of players. The Norwich fans were at the tunnel end, so we walked out to a cauldron of noise. It was something that, as a child and then as a footballer, I had always wished for.

But we lost the final, 1-0 to Tottenham, which is something I do look back on with disappointment. And we didn't win a single game between the semi-final and the final, which left us near the foot of the table.

In the end we scrambled to safety at the end of the season, and I scored the goal that kept us up. It was against Crystal Palace, at Carrow Road, in the last but one game of the season. It was the final match of the three-game Easter period, and it was between them and us for one of the relegation spots. We were drawing 1-1 with minutes to go and I flung myself at a corner and that was what kept us up. Staying up was a great satisfaction. We had spent so much emotion and energy that season.

But we struggled the following season, Ron left, and in came John Bond.

As people, Saunders and Bond were two different person-alities completely. Ron was very starchy. He didn't let anyone take any liberties. In fact he didn't really let anyone do anything. So we couldn't believe the freedom John gave us. He was very open and outgoing.

Part of his gambit, to raise the club's profile, was that he wanted to be in the limelight and take the club with him. So he told us it was perfectly fine for us to talk to the Press, which is something Ron wouldn't tolerate.

John's training sessions were a different style all together to all the fitness work and drills Ron had insisted on. John wanted more flair in the play, and where Ron had made us very regimented, John wanted us to express ourselves and use our own initiative. He wanted us to see things in our own mind, and play that way.

I think being so rigid under Ron was our downfall in the top division because we needed more flair to open teams up, combined with our discipline and work-rate.

John brought a lot of players in. He'd come to us from Bournemouth and virtually transferred the Bournemouth team up to Norwich. But he had the advantage of inheriting players who had the Saunders discipline.

He was able to add players like Ted MacDougall, Phil Boyer and Mel Machin, who had all been brought up with him at Bournemouth, and people like Martin Peters, who had been schooled alongside John at West Ham.

John and Ken Brown, his number two, had played alongside Bobby Moore at West Ham and had played the Ron Green-wood style, but I never thought playing under John would be difficult for me, because I enjoyed the way we were playing. And the manager was happy that Duncan and me should be the no-nonsense rock on which the team was built. He told us to play if we had time, but to defend without taking liberties when we needed to. The people around us were able to express themselves because we were doing the job we were.

John Bond couldn't keep us up in that 1973-74 season, but the following season we won promotion again and went back to Wembley – and faced Ron Saunders.

We had three good seasons in the League Cup. We went: final, semi-final and then final again. But Ron's record in those three seasons was even better: final, final, final. He took us to Wembley, then did the same with Manchester City and then completed the hat-trick with Aston Villa. And, sadly from our point of view, he won it with Villa, beating us 1-0.

We beat Manchester United over two legs in the semi-final but we disappointed ourselves in the final. The truth is that each time at Wembley we didn't perform. We were better than we showed on the day, which was horrible.

But this time, reaching Wembley did not seriously detract from our league form and we earned promotion and started the 1974-75 season back in the top tier.

I turned 30 two months into the season, but I was still very fit and thought I'd got a few more seasons left as a player.

I was up against some good players, of course. John picked me in centre-midfield one game at Anfield to man-mark Kevin Keegan. Thanks very much.

In 1976, after 13 years and 499 first team appearances at Norwich, I joined Cambridge United. I knew my time at the top was coming to an end, and I wanted to play regularly. It was a good move for me geographically, because I didn't have to move house. But I didn't go there for a holiday. I took playing for them as seriously as I always did and we had two promotions in my four seasons there.

I was allowed to train some of the week at Norwich. When

John left to become manager of Manchester City he took some of the coaches with him. But Ken Brown became Norwich manager and asked me if I would come back and take over the youth team. I jumped at it and I loved it.

In the 1982-83 season we managed to win the FA Youth Cup, and that was one of the best experiences I had at Norwich: to take those boys, help them develop and then win a major national trophy with them. We played some very, very good football. The only game we lost all season was away in an international tournament. Domestically, we were unbeaten and it was a source of great satisfaction.

There were 10,000 at Carrow Road for the first leg of the final, against Everton. We won 3-2. There were 15,000 at Goodison for the second leg. We lost 3-2. They won the toss for the right to hold the decider at Goodison, and there were 20,000 there. Young Paul Clayton scored for us, and that was the only goal.

It had been a marathon final, which made winning even better. Our team was captained by Mark Crowe and eight of them went on to play in the first team, including Jeremy Goss, Tony Spearing and Louie Donowa.

I stepped up to become reserve team manager, but I was reluctant to do that because it had been so rewarding working with the youth team.

Then, in May 1987, Mel Machin, who had been number two to Ken, left to manage Manchester City. For the 1987-88 season, Ken made me and David Williams joint first-team coaches and I have to say that, from the start, that didn't feel right. David was a very good coach, but neither of us really knew who should be doing what.

The results didn't go well, perhaps because the instructions to the players weren't clear. In the October, Ken was asked to step down as manager and I was thrown into the top job.

It was a volatile time. The chairman, Robert Chase, was very unpopular with supporters, and when I took over it was difficult to get the players away from that atmosphere and back on the right track.

The first thing we did was set the demarcation lines. I was manager. Dave Williams was coach, Mike Walker was reserve team coach and Keith Webb was in charge of the youth team. We all knew our jobs and what we should be doing.

At the time I took over, Steve Bruce was being sold to Man United. I didn't know anything about it until I got the job and Alex Ferguson was ringing me every day and Steve was knocking on my door every day.

So it left me needing a centre half and trying to get us out of the mess we were in. A board meeting was held at the Maid's Head hotel, away from the club. I told them we needed someone who would score goals. They asked me for a name. I told them, 'Robert Fleck.' We'd had scouting reports on him from Scotland and so the chairman and I went up to see him playing for Rangers, and we brought him back to Norwich with us on the plane the next day.

At his first training session, Flecky was such a bubbly character, and was zipping around so much in five-a-sides that the other players wanted to show they were as good as him. It lifted the whole situation.

I got John O'Neill from QPR as a replacement for Bruce, but he got injured in his first game in a tackle by Wimbledon's John Fashanu and never played again. Flecky got injured, too but we turned the season around and had three consecutive wins over the Christmas and New Year period. We won 2-1 at Derby and then beat Chelsea 3-0 and West Ham 4-1 at Carrow Road. That settled us down. There were 21 teams in the top division that season, because it was in the middle of a restructuring. We finished 14th.

Then we got in a few more players. For the next season we bought Andy Townsend, Malcolm Allen and Andy Linighan: decent players. We already had Ian Butterworth, and the boys from Spurs: Mark Bowen, Ian Culverhouse and Ian Crook. And we had Dale Gordon, Ruel Fox and Robert Rosario.

In that 1988-89 season we reached the FA Cup semi-final and finished fourth in the top division. In the semi-final, we lost to a Pat Nevin goal against Everton at Villa Park but our disappointment was put into proper perspective by the Hillsborough disaster that happened in the other semi-final on the same day. In the league, we really thought we had a chance to finish even higher, but the teams who finished above us were Arsenal, who took the title by winning at Anfield on the last day, Liverpool, who won the FA Cup, and Nottingham Forest, who won the League Cup.

Fourth place was the highest Norwich City had ever achieved at that time, and when I was asked to contribute to this book, I looked at some of the games on YouTube and thought, 'What on earth was I worried about? We played some brilliant football'.

I was lucky to have Dave Williams coaching. I gave him carte blanche on the training pitch while I got on with the other bits of being a manager, and I think that was something I needed to do: give him responsibility and the opportunity to prove his worth.

He was a very good coach, and we thought the same way about lots of things. He wasn't a yes-man. He was someone who would give me an argument if he thought it was necessary. But often I would say, 'I think we should make this change for Saturday' and he had already been thinking the same way.

I did find it stressful, though. The responsibility of it all was hard, because I loved the club and wanted it to do well. If I didn't care it wouldn't have mattered, but I did care about the club and everyone involved. I wanted to make sure that the people working with me were properly looked after, and so that was a responsibility as well.

At first I found it very, very difficult to cope because of the situation when I took over and all the animosity towards the chairman. I definitely lost sleep, and I was travelling all over the country looking at teams and players. I worked as hard as possible.

But after time, I became so used to the stress that sleep stopped being a problem but I still took all the responsibility very seriously. I didn't take it out on my wife and children or anything like that, but I did retreat into a world of my own at home. At the dinner table the conversation would go around the table but stop at me. I would be thinking about something involving my job.

I used to put players' names on pieces of paper and put them down in formations on the dining table – and my daughter, Louise, would come in and blow them all away, which was a bit of light in all the constant thinking about the club.

I look back and think that I did not do badly, and we reached the FA Cup semi-finals again in 1992. This time we were at Hillsborough. Our opponents, Sunderland, were in the division below us but, again, we lost 1-0.

And as the 1991-92 season came towards its end I knew it was time to step down. I think the players get too used to a particular manager saying the same things, and they needed a bit of a change.

I went to see the chairman and said, 'I'm going to resign at the end of the season.' We'd had a bad league season, but we made ourselves safe, so I went to him before the final game and told him the team needed to hear a new voice.

Mr Chase tried to persuade me not to go. He wanted me to stay. But I had made my mind up. He called a press conference

for the next day, but said that, at any time right until the conference started, I could change my mind.

I didn't. I had worked hard at a very stressful job and had
given everything to the club and what was important to me was
that it had not ended in failure. When I said, 'I'm resigning', I
felt such a sense of relief. It was like someone taking a weight
off the top of my head.

I think if I had gone on it would have been too long, and
I would not have got the response from the players that Mike
Walker got when he took over as manager.

I never left though. I was asked to help develop the new
training ground at Colney, so I went around the country, and
abroad, looking at other set-ups. I held meetings with architects
and so on. Then I came back into the club as assistant director
of the academy, and did a lot of the coaching – which is what
I enjoy.

I retired in 2002 but, on occasions, the board have asked me
for an input on appointments.

I am proud that I was never sacked. I served the club in a
long career and in a wide range of roles and I think I had a very
successful and satisfying career.

When people say to me, 'Don't you wish this or that?', I tell
them that I have no complaints about my time at Norwich. I
had so much enjoyment, fulfilment and, in lots of ways, success.

The thing that lots of people say is that if I was playing
now I'd be very comfortably off but that doesn't bother me. I
lived in a particular era and can't change that. Players like Terry
Allcock and others of his era might think my generation were
better off than they were. You just live and play when you do
and that doesn't bother me one bit.

Before this book comes out, my wife, Linda – a Gorleston
girl, of course – and I will celebrate our 50th wedding anniver-
sary. We still live near where we both grew up, and I am grateful

to Norwich City that they gave me the work that meant we didn't have to move away or traipse around the country moving every couple of years, like some players.

I have no regrets at all about my playing career. I played all those games for Norwich, stayed in the team for all those seasons, and the success came at the right time – when I was beginning to think I might have to move on to get to the top division. It was great to do it with Norwich. It is my home club. I still have that affection for them now. I get more nervous watching them from off the pitch than I did when I was involved.

Now on match days I do a little work with guests in hospitality at Carrow Road. In that role, it helps me that I have seen the club grow and seen the ground grow. I was there before we'd ever been in the top division. I remember the fire that destroyed the main stand. The ground is unrecognisable from what it was like when I stood on the terrace at the River End to watch games. Norwich City has grown from quite humble beginnings, really, to be the place and the club it is now, and when I talk to the guests about it I have the full history in my mind. It's easy for me because, I suppose, I am a part of that history.

Dave Stringer played 499 games for Norwich. He was voted player of the season as the club won promotion to the top tier for the first time and he played in City's first two Wembley finals. He coached the first group of City youngsters to win the FA Youth Cup and then had five seasons as first team manager, taking the side to two FA Cup semi-finals and to fourth place in the top division.

5

Kevin Bond gives a brutally frank assessment of what his own prospects would have been if his father had not been Norwich City manager.

But his self-deprecating tale has a cast of characters that includes some of the Canaries' all-time greats.

And, as the plot unfolds, the reader is reminded that the author became a lot more than just his daddy's boy.

STAYING OUT TO AVOID HOME TRUTHS

BY KEVIN BOND

I would not have had a career in football if it had not been for my dad, John Bond. He was the manager at Bournemouth who gave me an apprenticeship, and when he moved to Norwich he took me with him. Nobody else would have taken me on at that stage. I only got given a chance because of who my dad was. He presented me with the opportunity to learn to be a footballer, and my whole career – the playing and the coaching – came from that. I have always known that and never pretended otherwise.

People sometimes say to me that it must have been amazing growing up with my father being a player at West Ham and having the other players popping around all the time, but it wasn't really like that at all.

I went to Wembley for the 1964 FA Cup Final to watch dad play for West Ham against Preston. I wasn't quite seven, but I can just about remember it now.

But, to be honest, at that stage, there really didn't seem anything special about having a footballer for a dad. Players in those days were very much closer to the man in the street and weren't fêted like they are today. I never looked at him as doing anything special.

We lived in a terraced house in Fawn Road, no more than 400 yards from West Ham's ground, and we never thought of ourselves as any different to anyone else in the street and never got treated any differently. That's what it was like in those days.

Life was much more normal and low-profile for players.

But I do remember that, after my dad won the cup final, everyone had all the regalia out to greet him when he got home. That was the first time that I appreciated what he was and what the team had achieved. Even so, it wasn't until my father took charge at Bournemouth that things changed and he had a higher profile.

When he left West Ham, he had a couple of seasons at Torquay. We still lived in London, and he still trained with West Ham, but he would drive to Torquay on a Friday night for the next day's game. With no motorways, that was a six-hour journey. Imagine a footballer doing that now.

There was one time he left it until the Saturday morning to drive down. But the manager, Frank O'Farrell, found out and didn't pick him as a punishment. He never did that again.

Once he finished playing, dad did a bit of coaching at Gillingham for next to no money. He had to go through the old Dartford Tunnel and pay, and the amount he paid every day made a real dent in what they were giving him. Then, in May 1970, he became manager of Bournemouth and we moved down there. I was 12.

I'd played football for as long as I could remember. I would come home from school and, even as a six-year-old, go straight outside and play football wherever there was a piece of grass. It really was 'jumpers for goalposts'. We would stay there until it got dark and then go home. My parents didn't have to worry where I was, because it was completely safe. All the kids were out there playing football and there was a community spirit.

My son has never had one evening like that in his whole life because, with the traffic and with all the fears of what someone might come along and do, we just couldn't let him go off somewhere with a ball. So, unless there is an organised game or training session, kids don't play now.

What also used to happen was that, because the wages for footballers weren't anything special, players coached in schools a couple afternoons a week for a few quid. Most of the West Ham players did that and my father used to come and put on football sessions during PE lessons at the school I went to in Canning Town.

But mostly, I learned playing every night with my mates. I had years and years of playing football in the streets and, unbeknown to us, we improved and learned without even realising. The games were competitive too, and you started to have a streak of that in you as well.

By the time we moved to Bournemouth, I was playing for my school but I was absolutely not any great shakes at the game. I was very small then. I was about eight and a half stones and five feet five tall. And I don't think anyone would describe me as a natural athlete. So I know I got given one hell of an opportunity because my dad was manager of Bournemouth. I would never have been given it anywhere else or by anyone else.

My big break was that he took me on as an apprentice. Ultimately, when a club takes someone on as an apprentice, they are nearly always taking a punt. There are very few dead-certs. But nobody other than my dad would have even taken a punt on me. Physically I wasn't someone that anyone else would take a chance on. That's the truth.

My dad told me later that he saw something in me and he used to say that with young players, if there is just a glimmer there, it is something to build on. He thought I had an understanding of football – I could read the game – and he also believed I could pass. That was the long and the short of it.

When my father moved to Norwich, in 1973, I was in my first year of a three-year-apprenticeship at Bournemouth. They said they were happy to release me and they paid up the rest of my contract. So I got a cheque from Bournemouth for about

£240 and it was like a Pools win to me.

Dad said, 'Right, I'll take you on at Norwich'. So I served the last two years of my apprenticeship at Norwich.

Of course there must have been people at Norwich City who thought that wasn't right, and I am sure there were some saying, 'This boy is never going to make it.' But I was very naïve and I was oblivious to all that, if it was going on. If I had been aware of it at that stage, I think it would have really hurt me and it might have been too much for me. But because, in my ignorance, it was all going straight over my head, I just carried on and, on the surface, everyone was as good as gold to me.

My dad had given me this big chance, but neither he nor anyone else at the club gave me any special treatment as an apprentice. I wasn't exactly setting the world alight, though.

George Lee looked after the apprentices. He was a wiry little bloke who had served in the Second World War and then played for West Brom in the 1954 FA Cup Final. He'd been at Norwich about ten years before my father took over and dad kept him on.

George coached the Norwich City 'A' team, who played in the Eastern Counties League. I was still very small, and that was a men's league. We were professionals and the teams playing us were semi-pro at best and they did take a delight in getting one over on us. They usually did too. We would get beaten nearly every week. And every Monday morning for about a year my dad would ask how we'd got on, and George would tell him. Then dad would ask, 'How did Kevin do?' Week after week, game after game, George would reply, 'He never got a kick'. He was completely honest.

My dad wasn't bothered about the results. He wanted all the youth team players to be giving all they had to give and to be improving – and that was what he wanted for and from me.

We didn't have any of the facilities that clubs have now. The training ground was at Trowse, and there was only one pitch, which used to get badly cut up. George used to take us away to some part of the ground and have us jumping over sticks and things like that. In fact, we were doing exactly the exercises that players do now, but in a much more primitive form. George had to improvise instead of having state-of-the-art equipment.

I loved it. And the best thing about that period for me was that one day on the bus in Cringleford I met a young lady. It turned out she lived about 100 yards from our family. Tina became my wife, and we have two children, Jack and Lily. I have Norwich to thank for my gorgeous family.

But there came a time, towards the Christmas of my last year as an apprentice, when my father sat me down at home one evening and said, 'Kevin, unless you improve, I am going to have to let you go in the summer'.

Knowing my dad, that wouldn't have been an easy thing to say to his son. But we'd reached the point where, for him, as manager of Norwich City, I had to start showing something more or he just couldn't take me on. In all seriousness, however much he loved me, he could not put his reputation and perhaps his job at risk by having me there as a full professional if I wasn't up to it. And, actually, he wouldn't be doing me any favours, let alone himself, if he had continued to support me when I had no chance. He had gone so far, and given me the opportunity, but if I couldn't make the most of it then he would have to say, 'Kevin, we are going to have to end this.'

That little Christmas talk was a massive kick up the backside for me. A lot of young footballers think it is a natural progression. You get an apprenticeship and then, at the end of it, you're going to get a one or two-year professional contract. But obviously lots don't. They fall by the wayside and I realised I was in danger of having that happen to me.

So I did definitely buck my ideas up and I had a growth

spurt too. So, in the summer, I did get a contract.

At that stage at the club, we had the likes of Justin Fashanu breaking through, we had Greg Downs coming through,
and my dad had signed two young strikers: Kevin Reeves from
Bournemouth and Roger Gibbins from Oxford. It was a really
good crop of young players.

Justin, of course, was phenomenal at Norwich and became
a million-pound player. Greg started out as a striker but converted to left back and, after Norwich, he won the FA Cup
with Coventry. I was really pally with Roger, who had been an
England schoolboy and started his career with Spurs. But my
biggest mate was Kevin.

He had been an apprentice at Bournemouth, a year behind
me, and he and I were already mates when he arrived in Norwich. When my dad paid £50,000 for him, you couldn't have
guessed that he would eventually go to Manchester City for
£1.25 million – the first seven-figure fee Norwich ever got.
After a difficult start at Norwich, he kicked on and you could
see that he was a really clever, bright player. I was at Wembley,
supporting him, when he won his first England cap in bizarre
circumstances in November 1979.

England were playing Bulgaria at Wembley in a European
qualifier and the game was supposed to be on the Wednesday
night, as was usually the case then. But on the night, there was
thick fog and they didn't even attempt to start the game. Instead, they rearranged it for the following night.

But Kevin Keegan, who was just about the most famous
footballer on the planet, couldn't hang around for an extra 24
hours because he had to report back to his club, Hamburg. And
it was Norwich City's Kevin Reeves who took his place in the
team. He won one more cap once he had moved to Manchester
City. When he finished playing, it was my father who gave him
his first coaching job, at Birmingham.

In my father's time, young players were encouraged at Norwich and eased towards the first team. He would take us away on pre-season tours to give us game-time. He would take one or two on the odd first team away trip just for the experience. And, at the end of a season, if there was nothing at stake, he'd put youngsters into the first team.

These days, managers can't really do that. In the Premier League, there is a huge amount of money involved according to exactly where you finish in the table. And in the lower divisions, with play-offs, lots of clubs still have something to play for right up to the end of the season.

But there wasn't too much riding on the last few results for Norwich at the end of the 1975-76 season, and so the very first time I got onto the pitch for the first team was in April 1976, at Leicester City. I came on as a sub for the last 20 minutes. I never touched the ball but when I came off I was completely drained because of all the nervous energy I had expended. All the boys laughed their socks off because they'd played a full game and I'd played less than a quarter of it, hadn't got a touch, but was the most knackered.

It was another year before I started a match, though: at Aston Villa in the game that Billy Steele, a really promising midfielder, had his career effectively ended by a knee injury.

And it wasn't until the 1977-78 season that I made my breakthough. John Ryan was the right back, but I got a game because he was injured and then, when he was available again, he was given a run in midfield and he was a real success there, banging in goals from 40 yards or so. He ended the season as our top scorer with 16 goals. 'Ryno' certainly didn't mind that I had taken over at right back. We became good friends. I am godfather to one of his children and I used to go to his house sometimes when the going got too tough at home.

We lived in Cringleford: dad, my mum Janet, me and my

sister Toni. Football was all-consuming in our household. Once I was in the team, if we'd lost, I'd go out after a game and not go home until I was pretty sure dad would be in bed. That was how it was. There was no escape if I went home and he was still up. There would be a long, long conversation about the game and it would inevitably lead back to me and my performance and dad didn't hold back. He would pick my game apart. He was fair in what he said but, for other players, their home was somewhere they could get away from football and talk about other things. For me it was worse at home than anywhere else.

My dad would encourage me too. He would always tell me when I did something well, but he wouldn't leave a stone unturned if he thought I should have done better and he would be brutally honest with me and give me both barrels.

Fortunately, we won a few games! And I did okay too.

I won two England 'B' caps while at Norwich – against New Zealand and Australia. Glenn Hoddle was in the team and so was Glenn Roeder. I even scored a few goals for Norwich. I got 11 in the 1979-80 season, and was second highest scorer behind Justin Fashanu. I was the penalty taker, which explains some of them, but I used to get some others. At the start of that season, I got what I think was my best ever goal, in a 2-1 win at home to Leeds. It was from outside the box, but I can't trace any video footage of it to show anyone how good it was!

I became captain and I was voted player of the 1979-80 season, which must mean that by then the supporters weren't complaining that it was my dad selecting me. And I have the Football Association to thank for one of my Norwich achievements that same campaign. I hadn't missed a League game but picked up too many bookings and was going to get a ban near the end of the season. In those days you could appeal, so I did, and I said to the disciplinary commission that I had this opportunity to complete a whole League season without missing a game, and they let me off with a warning.

At Norwich in that era we held our own in the top division. Dad won promotion for only the second time in the club's history, kept us up and, I believe, set the club on course for a long period of stability in the top tier. After he took us up, Norwich spent 16 of the next 18 seasons in the top tier.

In his time, Norwich held their own against teams with some very good players. Liverpool were all-conquering then, and playing them was always very difficult, but, them apart, we used to give as good as we got. We lost games we shouldn't have but we won games people didn't expect us to. And in the time that I was there, and my dad was in charge, we always ended the season pretty comfortably established in what was the equivalent of today's Premier League.

When I was right back for Norwich, Jimmy Neighbour was most often the player in front of me in the 4-4-2 formation. What a player he was. We had some other good players too though. Alongside me in defence were people like David Jones and Tony Powell. In midfield was Mick McGuire and, before my time in the first team but while I was at the club, there was Ted MacDougall and Phil Boyer in attack. Later on there was Joe Royle, who I learned a lot from, but the most amazing player during my time at Carrow Road was Martin Peters.

Apart from my dad, Martin was the biggest influence on me as a player. Just being there and seeing how he conducted himself, and watching how he did things on and off the pitch taught me a lot.

It was only just over ten years earlier that he had been in the England team who won the World Cup, and he scored in the final. So of course he had something special about him.

He was such an intelligent player and I really liked him as a guy. Training in the morning started at 10 o'clock, but we would be out 15 minutes earlier chipping balls between each other.

When we played eight-a-side games, he would play at centre back every single time and, believe me, he could have played there comfortably at the very highest level because he could read the game brilliantly.

In matches, he was class. He had no real pace and he wasn't particularly strong – although he could be nasty if he needed to be – but he was a midfielder with perfect timing. He would just arrive in the right place at the right moment. That's how he got his goals. He would be there at the perfect time. He read the game and was a move ahead of everyone and always looked as if he had all the time in the world on the ball. Yes, class.

The pub the players used to drink in was the Murderers, in Timber Hill. All the lads would have a pint of lager and lime, but on the odd occasion Martin would join us, he would have a half. At the end of the evening he would have drunk as much as anyone else, but the difference in the perception of someone drinking halves was the thing. So, before very long, all the lads would have halves – not because he'd told us to, but we had all watched him and followed his example.

Martin was part of what was an exceptional set of senior players. I still keep in touch with Kevin Keelan, who holds the record for Norwich appearances. He was a big character as well as a big goalkeeper. He is still a goalkeeping coach in Florida, although he is well into his seventies.

Duncan Forbes was immense. I have never met a greater guy and he was so funny. He used to say he had only ever been carried off once: shoulder high. He was a proper man. So was Dave Stringer, who was brilliant with me, a youngster, when he was someone who had already been there years and years.

Ryno and Tony Powell were jokers, and really good to have in the dressing room. Mel Machin and John Benson, who played for dad at Bournemouth and Norwich, and followed him into coaching, were big influences too, and it was Benno who said to my dad, 'Have you thought of playing Kevin at centre half?' It had certainly never crossed my mind, but after Benno had said that, I played at centre half in the reserves a couple of times, and it became my position. Ken Brown, whose own son Kenneth (who is ten years younger than me) was trying to become a professional footballer – and of course did – so Ken senior really understood my situation and was very supportive. I don't think any of these people had an issue with who I was.

My father didn't like how it ended for him at Norwich. It upset certain elements at Norwich that he was going to Manchester City and he didn't leave on the terms he would have liked to. That got to him. On one occasion, at home, I saw him crying. In later life, dad said he made a mistake leaving Norwich when he did. In hindsight he realised that the working relationship he had with the chairman, Sir Arthur South, was special. My father was offered a ten-year contract and could have stayed and been perfectly happy. But at the time, as an ambitious man, he felt he had to take the job that was offered to him by Peter Swales, the Manchester City chairman. I think that is what most football people would have felt in the circumstances.

When my father left, everyone thought it would be difficult for the ex-manager's son to still be at Norwich. I stayed until the end of the season, but dad wanted me to go with him to Manchester and, to be perfectly honest, it suited me to go there. It wouldn't have looked right if I'd just breezed along after him, so I went to America to play for Seattle Sounders. Ryno had played for them the previous summer, and I'd gone out to the States to visit him and had actually trained with the team. So when it was clear I was going to leave Norwich, Alan Hinton, who was the manager in Seattle, said, 'Come out and play for me'. Football was doing well in the US at that time and we had some good players, including Bruce Rioch, and good crowds.

I stayed out there until the September and then, of course, I did go to Manchester City, for a tidy sum of money. It was the 1981-82 season. I was reunited with my father, but by then I had a solid reputation as a defender and so I don't believe there was any suggestion of nepotism at all.

I had three good seasons, and then moved on to Southampton and had four seasons there. The next stop was back to where my football career had begun, Bournemouth, then on to Exeter before I wound down my playing days at Sittingbourne and Dover Athletic. Ryno was the manager at both those clubs.

I have had too many coaching jobs to go into here, but during that part of my career, I would have to say Harry Redknapp has been the biggest influence on me. I worked with him at West Ham, Southampton, Portsmouth, Tottenham and QPR – so he had plenty of opportunities to influence me!

But my first coaching influence was dad. He wasn't one for sitting in an office if there was training going on. He would be out there with his boots on. Different managers have different approaches to the job, but dad was a coach as well as a manager.

I'd like to think he was proud that I have had some top coaching roles and I do believe he was proud of what I achieved as a player. I never won any silverware, but if I analyse it, for me to clock up more than 560 senior games after really struggling when I was starting out I think I did well. I hope my father felt I repaid him for the huge opportunity he gave me.

Kevin Bond joined Norwich as an apprentice when his father, John, became manager in 1974. By the time he left in 1981, he had been player of the season, scored 14 goals in 161 appearances and established himself as a top defender.

6

She launched a football magazine that became a global brand. But being a football journalist placed a strain on friendships and got in the way of supporting Norwich City.

Karen Buchanan had the sort of career many covet, and it gave her inside knowledge of events at Carrow Road.

But all she really wanted to do was take her place in the Snake Pit and make a noise for the boys.

LET ME HAVE MY PIT STOP

BY KAREN BUCHANAN

I didn't like being a football journalist. An odd thing to say when you've started a football magazine, written about football for national newspapers, written one football book, edited another and reported on a World Cup for *Match of the Day*. (Not to mention the small matter of baiting Ipsh*t fans on national and local radio stations – okay, that bit I rather enjoyed!).

But I don't think I was ever really cut out to be a football journalist, let alone a football reporter. I liked writing about football, but I never *covered* it. There is a big difference. The latter requires you to be analytical, up-to-date and fairly impartial; the other lets you do smart-ass jokes about haircuts, and muse out loud about what one would really do if one had the wings of a sparrow and the derrière of a crow.

One lets you have Saturdays off to watch football at the hallowed ground; the other requires you to work Saturdays and go to stupid grounds on the other side of the country. One requires you to know stuff and have lightning reflexes so you can note down who played the final ball in, whilst simultaneously tweeting it. The other allows you to go to the pub before and after the game, moan like hell about the ref and wallow in ecstasy/misery entirely untroubled by the need to attempt rational analysis.

Besides, I just don't have the ability to remember stats. I'm in good company. I once interviewed then-Liverpool manager Roy Evans for *FourFourTwo* and we sat in silence for what seemed like minutes while he tried to remember, 'Who did we play last Saturday?' Buggered if I knew!

But my lack of appetite for stats wasn't the main problem. It was the fact that a little knowledge can be a dangerous thing: knowledge that comes because you've met people and they trust you and they open up to you. Which is what we journalists do. We get to know people and gain their trust. We use this in all manner of ways to get a story and, until I started writing about football, I had no problem with that. It's entirely legitimate to do it; we mostly use that privileged information for the common good and I have always felt part of an honourable profession. I still do. I've been very lucky: my career has brought me many unique experiences, which I treasure. However, over the years, writing about the game I love has made me increasingly uncomfortable and changed my whole experience of watching footie.

I got into football via Italia '90 (yes, yes, I fell in love with Gazza's brilliance and *Nessun Dorma*'s grandeur, but I also loved the idea of a sport in which someone as banal as David Platt could be a national hero). I was completely hooked, although my first live football game wasn't until February 1991. England beat Cameroon 2-0 on a freezing cold night. It was the old Wembley and the old fences were still up. We sat in the gods, and I could hardly see.

My first Norwich game should have been at Highbury on August 15, the opening day of the 1992-93 season, but for some reason which eludes me I decided not to go. I have few regrets in my life: that decision was one; punching the air in our low-ceilinged basement flat in Brixton as City's fourth goal went in is definitely another.

My first game at Carra Rud? Can't actually remember. Some time that season, but it would have been in the Nice and Peaceful End, so I was probably asleep. But I do remember that, in

wakeful moments, I was loving the singing I could hear coming from the other end; loving the chanting; the pride and the
passion; the sense of belonging; of being part of something
special. And, as a journalist, I loved the fact that everything
rhymed. Often very badly, which just added to the brilliance.

I went to lots of games that season – home and away. I
sat in the River End (too quiet), and the South Stand (yup!),
and fleetingly considered sitting in the Main Stand (whatever it's
called) but thought better of it. Finally, I discovered the Snake
Pit where I had many happy, noisy, boisterous games until the
'No Surrender to the IRA' boys started really pissing me off
and I moved to the Lower Barclay. I've been there ever since
apart from once, when I left it so late to get tickets for a Chelsea
cup game we had to sit in the South Stand near the River End
corner flag. When Jimmy Floyd Hasselbaink came over to take
a corner, me and my other half shouted, 'Who are ya, who are
ya!', as is the custom, at which an older chap behind me tapped
me on the shoulder to inform me, 'Scuse me love. Thassss Jimmy Floyd Hasselbaink!'.

Sigh.

There should be signs up in the Lower Barclay to inform
you that you are now entering a foreign land where NOT
SINGING IS A CRIME. Seriously, it really gets my goat when
fans in the Lower Barclay choose to display their support for the
club by not singing. You have three other sides of the ground
to stage a silent protest from! And the Upper Barclay! And yet,
week after week, there you are, sitting in my eye-line, and when
we have a corner at our end and you can't get yourself excited
enough to even shout, 'Come On You Yellows!'

Maybe the nay-says are frightened of singing out of key
and being chastised for it by the Canary Fairy, or maybe they're
frightened of getting the words wrong (on one of my first
visits to Carra Rud I made the mistake of singing *Come On You*

Yellows rather lustily, at which point another old bloke behind me tapped me on the shoulder and said: 'Scuse me, thassss Yallooos'. True story). Anyway, if you're a football supporter: sing your heart out for the lads. Supporters actively support – and that means making some goddamn noise!

Ooh, the years of post-match ranting on *Wrath of the Barclay* just came flooding back then!

Part of the reason I came up with the idea of *FourFourTwo* was that there was very little in the papers about the mighty NCFC. We weren't considered newsworthy, despite the fact that that season we were doing a Leicester. One of our brilliant fanzines changed its name from *Liverpool Are On the Telly* Again to *Manchester United Are On the Telly Again*. The only Norwich stories in the nationals were sensationalised gossip and rumour. I, as a new convert, was desperate for information, rather than speculation. And I wanted to learn about the beautiful game. At the time, newspapers didn't have as much analysis of the game as they do now and the only magazines around were for children – *Match* and *Shoot!* I wanted more.

Already a journalist on the glamorous weekly business magazine *PrintWeek*, I was invited to lunch by my Spurs-supporting boss at Haymarket Publishing, Simon Kanter, where I suggested the idea of a football magazine for grown-ups – a monthly, glossy magazine with great photography that took fans places that were otherwise inaccessible; great writing; insightful, detailed interviews delving into players and managers' minds; witty pub repartee.

The launch was a big success and during the first year of the magazine we managed to build sales dramatically, due in part, I'm sure, to an exponentially increasing number of articles about Norwich City.

As a fan, I got to go places I'd never been before, which was illuminating, fascinating and, well, just brilliant. I went pre-season training with the Liverpool team (lovely breakfast at Melwood, nice little jog, bit of banter with the team and the tea ladies, afternoon spent in the hotel having a swim and watching telly; one of my toughest assignments). I got tired and emotional with Bazza Fry; I made Darren Eadie one of our first *Boy's A Bit Specials*. We went to El Tel's nightclub and hung out with Ian Wright Wright Wright. We went to the Sky Sports Awards and watched, in awe, as all the big-name players around us whispered to each other, 'Don't look now, but Kenny Dalglish's behind you!'

Then Norwich lost the final game of the 1994-95 season, at Leeds, and were relegated. I had never covered a Norwich game, but I had interviewed some of the players and, by coincidence, I was due to interview Robert Chase at Carra Rud on the Monday. My other half and I and our friend Sarah drove up to Leeds from London on the Friday night. She's from near Leeds and had invited us up for a big party to celebrate her 30th. At the final whistle, disgusted, dejected and furious, we stood and protested like many other fans.

Of course, we didn't have mobile phones in those days, so it wasn't until I got back to London early on the Monday morning to find an answerphone message from my mum that I realised something might be wrong. Cryptically, the message said, 'I always wanted a daughter, not a football hooligan!' I rang mum. She said, 'You're in the paper!'

The *Eastern Daily Press* had a huge photo all over the back page of myself and the boyfriend with fists clenched, shouting 'CHASE OUT!' Sarah, arms folded aggressively, scowling, looked every inch the disenchanted Norwich fan. (She isn't and was actually muttering, 'Come on you selfish swines. It's my bloody birthday – let's go!')

As I made my way to Carrow Road, I hoped that Chase hadn't seen the photo. I wondered whether to wear a moustache in case he had. When I got to the club Chase was sitting in one of the smaller function rooms and a camera crew from Anglia were setting up. He had a couple of finance people at what looked like a cards table — green baize, square and very small. He was in full flow and barely acknowledged me as he invited me to pull up a chair at the tiny table. He was having lunch and offered me some, bizarrely, from his plate. I was starving, but the idea of being given food from Robert Chase's plate was just too freakish. The idea of being filmed by Anglia TV accepting food from Robert Chase's plate was hideous. I was not that starving.

He never mentioned whether he'd seen the photo, but he turned in his chair, stared at me and said, 'What am I supposed to have done?'

Without thinking, the words just slipped out: 'I'll tell you what you've done!' followed by a rather flustered: 'Errr, Norwich fans tell me that they blame you for the club being relegated.'

It was one of the most uncomfortable interviews of my life. I have the greatest respect for my print, radio and TV colleagues who cover their local team or cover a particular team. It's extremely hard to do so without getting involved. I loved hearing Chris Goreham's impassioned commentaries when Norwich City were flying up the League – for me, that's how it should be. And he does all that, live, without swearing! I couldn't do it.

It's much easier to comment on, pontificate about, be objective about a club that isn't yours, a love that isn't yours. Over the course of my career, the more professionally involved with Norwich I've got, the more difficult I've found being a fan. For me, they have to be very separate things. Sometimes it's fantastic to meet your heroes. Sometimes it's a let-down. Sometimes you find out things that change your view of a person or situation.

Take Sooper Matty Jackson – at the time one of my all-time heroes and venerated in my imagination as A Damn Fine Bloke. I was at Colney to see someone and was sitting in the canteen talking to Keith O'Neill about him being injured. Sooper Matty came over and butted into our conversation. My initial pleasure at meeting him quickly turned to disgust.

'Well, you don't really care about it though do you Keith?'

'Er, yes, yes I do!'

'Well, I wouldn't. I mean, you still get paid either way and at least this way you don't have the fans on your back, moaning. It's easy money…'

I was devastated. My hero – and he didn't care a bit! He didn't give two hoots for us fans! He went on in this manner for another couple of minutes, before suddenly turning to me. 'You should see your face! It's a picture!', he said and burst out laughing.

The famous bants. I'll forgive him one day, the sod…

Then there was the day I received an invite to go to dinner with Delia Smith. I had just written an editor's letter for *FourFourTwo* about my New Year resolutions, which included 'buying a copy of Delia's *Winter Collection* to say thank you for saving my club'. A week or two later, a package arrived containing a copy of the *Summer Collection* and a card that read: 'As you already have winter, thought you might like a copy of the summer collection. Michael and I would be delighted if you would join us for supper to share hopes and dreams. Delia'.

I immediately flew into a panic. For a start, I had not actually bought the Winter Collection and my culinary skills were restricted to opening a jar of Dolmio. The second point of panic was that I was a foul-mouthed, chain-smoker who liked a glass or three of wine (I've changed now. I don't smoke.) How could I possibly go for dinner at the house of one of the world's greatest cooks; indeed, the home of the woman the nation's tabloids called Saint Delia? I remember putting off accepting the invite for quite a while, as I was so nervous: what to wear, whether to curtsey?!

But my other half and I did make the long drive from south-west London to the Norfolk-Suffolk border where Delia and Michael live. There had been a crash on the North Circular, so we rather foolishly decided to go on the M25. Three hours later we were at Colney (the London training ground of Arsenal, not our one). Of course, this being the late 1990s, we didn't have mobile phones, so we kept turning off the main road in search of a payphone that hadn't been vandalised. If we'd just driven straight there rather than phoning to apologise for our lateness I'm sure we would have been there in time for the main course.

As it was, we arrived after everyone had finished eating. They had saved some for us though and Delia and Michael immediately relaxed us by joking that they would have been done for murder if they'd had to endure a six-hour drive from London. We talked football and sang, making up our own chants about how Norwich City players gave us Fever. 'O'Neill lights up the left side, Eadie lights up the right, I light up when you score a goal, You give me fever right through the night'. We were still singing when the dawn made the sky go appropriately yellow.

Delia and Michael are two of the most passionate, knowledgeable, hard-working, dedicated, caring, funny, thoughtful people I know. They cannot get it right all of the time; nobody does. It grieves me when people make ill-informed comments about them; that is part of the reason I'm glad I'm no longer a football journalist. It's hard to hear hurtful comments about people you love.

Some time after I first met Delia and Michael and just before the fabulous Andy Cullen came on the scene I was asked to do some marketing for the club on a freelance basis. I launched myself into it with great enthusiasm, loads of ideas and not much experience. At the time our average gate was around 15,000, and I wanted a few more of the 'I'll start going when we start winning' types to sign up.

So I created a *Bluffer's Guide to Norwich City*, with the aim of giving it to all new and potential fans. I think one of the big barriers to anyone's engagement in sport is not understanding it – not just the rules, but the jokes, the rhythms, the banter. It made page three of the *EDP* and was deemed a big success. I designed a well-received range of Christmas cards, including a photo of a gap-toothed smiling Iwan and an ode to the little lord Eadie laying down his sweet head. And I started writing a column in the programme under the dynamic title: A View From the Barclay. (To those who keep asking: I was NEVER Aunt Erica!)

My first programme column talked about playing Nobbies and Stobbies on the road to away games and drew an encouraging response. My second banged my favourite noisy-but-not-in-an-annoying-Sheffield-Wednesday-way drum about how only one side of the ground sings. I jokily offered to give a fiver to charity if I heard the South Stand sing. And a tenner if the River End sang up.

A week later the Man In the Stands had a go at me. For those too young to remember, MITS was a column in the much-lamented weekly *Pink Un*, the Saturday evening newspaper covering the Canaries, published by Archant and then edited by Joe Ferrari (now the esteemed PR Mafioso at Carra Rud). The *Pink Un* was the highlight of the week as it came out within an hour or two of the final whistle, complete with match report, from THAT DAY, which was AMAZING! You guys with this internet thing, you don't know you're born!

MITS wrote a witty, acerbic collection of stories and gossip, but never revealed his name. That week he wrote a rather horrible piece about me which went something like,

'Hey! Look at me! I'm a girl and a friend of Delia's and I've taken a break from eating cranberries to write a programme column to tell everyone off for not making any noise! Get back to your prawn sandwiches love.'

It probably wasn't as well-written as that, but his sneers seemed a bit harsh and personal and I'm ashamed to say I burst into tears. After much deliberation, I decided to front it up and the next week I marched (if you can march when you're shaking with nerves) into the Archant offices demanding to see MITS. Of course, he wasn't there, so Joe Ferrari came to meet me. He seemed even more nervous than me. I handed him a cheque (ask your parents) for £10 made payable to Man In The Stands, with a note saying, 'Nice to hear someone in the River End finally making some noise!' The next week Man In the Stands ran a story apologising and saying I was a top bird.

I had left *FourFourTwo* by then to go freelance and had started writing for the *Daily Telegraph*. For about six months I wrote a main feature for their Monday edition. But they started sending me to all sorts of odd places to cover games (not my forte, due to my tendency to get over-excited). I remember being at countless different grounds watching games and caring only about finding out the Norwich result (on a telly in the press lounge or manager's room afterwards). I had a sort of football Tourette's: I knew I should be asking questions about their win, but instead, 'Do you know how Norwich got on?' invariably slipped out.

That said, I did see some great games: AFC Sudbury v Sudbury Town in the cup was amusing as they were both home and away at the same time. I can't remember which Sudbury won, but I recall that the entire town piled into the clubhouse for an almighty piss-up.

Writing for the *Telegraph* and working for Norwich City was fun but it meant I was missing out on doing what I loved: going to the football. If I was working for the *Telegraph*, I was feigning interest at some other fixture. If I was working for Norwich I had responsibilities at the club, sometimes before the game, sometimes after the game. The problem with either was my temperament. Before football I'm stupidly excited and after football I'm either really high or I'm really low. You know what I'm talking about: when you're so exhausted after an exciting/frustrating/tedious game that you can't summon up the energy to even say hello to anyone, let alone be polite to them or take part in a sensible conversation! (After the 7-1, my friend and I sat in silence for two whole pints before we managed to form words. Four-lettered ones.)

There was also the problem that I now knew too much. Granted, that's not an accusation that's been levelled at me frequently, but working at the club made me privy to certain information which I couldn't share with my friends over our pre-match moan. It was very frustrating as Lisa, Jen, Gavin and Cookie sat there and asked me what was going on and I knew and couldn't tell them.

I wanted to be free to sit and debate the finer points of Keith Scott with the best of them. So, I was glad when the *Telegraph*'s new sports ed brought in his own first XI of writers and I was glad to step down from my small marketing role when the much more capable Mr Cullen came along. I was able to be a proper fan again.

A few years later, an old pal of mine, Jim Drewett, got in touch to ask me to write a football book for his brand new publishing company. 'If you were going to write a book about one Norwich player, who would it be?' he asked.

"EWWWWWWWWWWW-ANNNNNNNN!" I replied.

Writing a book with Iwan was a dream. My first meeting with him was hilarious. The combination of my nerves, an extreme lack of fitness, a very hot day and my 20-a-day habit meant that I was struggling for breath by the time I mounted three flights of stairs to meet him. He spotted me before I had a chance to compose myself so his first impression of me would have been of a rather sweaty heavy-breather. Why he agreed to do the book, I have no idea.

We agreed to meet once a week; Iwan would 'do his home-work' and write down what he'd been up to every day and I would 'check his homework' and interview him about it. There were two problems. One was that Iwan's such a nice bloke. The other was that he mentioned Delaney's bar so often people would wonder if the book was sponsored.

I remember meeting up with him at the Rushcutters pub in Norwich one week, a few months into our diary of the season. I read his notes and stared at him.

'So you were quite happy about being dropped for the West Ham game then?' I asked.

'Are you having a laugh? I was gutted!'

'But your notes don't mention it at all!' I pointed out.

'I didn't think you'd want stuff about that,' he said.

'Well, it's a change from Delaney's!' I said.

When the book was published, Norwich City only agreed to stock it in their club shops if they could be sure there was nothing in it that would offend or embarrass anyone connected to the club. Fair enough, I suppose. So we agreed that I would print out the relevant pages where Iwan slated the then manager Nigel Worthington for dropping him and take them to Colney to show Nigel. Standing in front of him while he read the parts where Iwan says, 'he let me down, handled it badly, ranted and raved', was the longest 20 minutes of my life. There were some harsh sentiments. Eventually Nigel turned over the last page.

'Well, you didn't dress it up and you didn't dress it down.' I remember saying that and I remember him being bitterly disappointed I'd dropped him. Fair play. I'm happy.'

To me, his honest, straightforward reaction says a lot about the man. I was desperately sad to see him go. I thought we played some amazing football under him (the Burnley 5-3 away day and the players' and Nigel's reactions afterwards particularly stay in my mind) and I was disgusted that he was effectively forced out by an evil atmosphere that built inside Carra Rud and created a self-fulfilling prophecy. I think he deserved another season. He was a decent man.

The book led to an appearance on BBC Radio Norfolk's *The Scrimmage* to publicise it. Matthew Gudgin told me, 'You're a natural; you should come and do some news shifts for us. We'll be in touch.'

A year later the phone rang.

'Can you come in tomorrow?'

'Err… okay.'

My very first sports bulletin, back in 2006, was memorable for two reasons. The lunchtime show presenter, Tony Mallion, would be in the main studio, while the sports news person was in a little news studio. You could see each other via TV screens and talk to each other via a talkback system. Tony saw that I was in the studio ready to go and introduced me.

'Now here's Karen Buchanan with the sports news.'

I began reading my well-rehearsed script as clearly and confidently as possible, while shaking uncontrollably with nerves. It seemed to be going well. I hadn't mispronounced any of the names or made any slip-ups… hang on… Tony seemed to be saying something… 'Well, Karen *will* be bringing you your sports news once she's worked out she has to push the little fader button up so you can hear her talk!'

The next outing wasn't much better. The BBC's central sports team sends regional stations audio clips of national stories – interviews with the England manager, tennis players and so on – which the stations are free to use as they wish in their bulletins. In those days you had to convert them into a different format otherwise they might not play or might play at twice the speed. My top story was that Wolverhampton manager Mick McCarthy and Sunderland manager Roy Keane were set to put their differences behind them ahead of a big league meeting between the two. (They had famously fallen out at the 2002 World Cup in Japan).

I read my cue...

'Mick McCarthy says they've buried the hatchet and he's looking forward to seeing Roy Keane again...'

And pressed play...

Mickey Mouse's voice squeaked, double-speed, something unintelligible, the only discernible words being Roy and Keane.

I panicked. I didn't know how to get it to play correctly. Should I acknowledge it or just move on? Eventually, I stopped the audio and said, as calmly as possible:

'Mick McCarthy there, talking about meeting up with Roy Keane again. As you can tell, he's really rather excited about it!'

During my six years with Radio Norfolk, I was lucky enough to work with some brilliant people and do all sorts of interviews ranging from a discussion about suicide amongst farmers to running a three-legged race with the divine Rick Wakeman.

But the absolute highlight, the absolute favourite thing I think I have ever done in my life is mercilessly ripping the mick out of Ipswich Town fans after beating them. There was the day I decided to only play songs relating to the word Five, the day all songs had to be green or yellow, the 9-2 day. Oh what fun we had! Editor David Clayton gave me permission to camp it up; the suggestions from listeners came thick and fast. We were all revelling in it; loving it. As Norwich fans we know you have to enjoy it while you can. So, it was utterly self-indulgent, but everyone listening was loving it. Apart from one man who texted: 'You have to understand that not all BBC Radio Nor-folk listeners are Norwich fans; some of us are Ipswich fans!'

I read out his text and pointed out to the listener that there was indeed a radio station for people like him: it was called BBC Radio *Suffolk*. And I suggested he listen to that as at BBC Radio *Norfolk*, we supported our local team, funnily enough. There was a bit of a clue in the name...

I got another text.

'This is getting very boring. If you carry on like this I'm switching to BBC Radio 2.'

I asked the listeners if I was being boring and had gone too far. They replied, rather emphatically, that I was only just getting started.

A few minutes later I got another text:

'I'm switching to Radio 2 now!' I mourned his loss and played another track by FiveStar.

And a few minutes later: 'You're being very silly and childish.'

Yes, I was. And he was still listening, obviously.

Teasing Ipswich fans is enormous fun. But I didn't enjoy the times I was asked (not unreasonably) to report on Nor-wich City in a more formal manner or the (less reasonable) way some people tried to exploit my friendships to get extra access to the club. The quality of my friendships with people is everything to me and there were times, as most journalists will have experienced, where I felt compromised, where I felt I was being asked to betray confidences, rather than 'merely' abuse my friendships.

I never did betray those confidences, but I'm sure my rela-tionships with various football people have improved since I stopped having a professional opinion on the football on my doorstep. I greatly admire the likes of Chris Goreham, Matt Gudgin, Phil Daley, Richard Hancock and the rest of the BBC

Radio Norfolk sports team who can forge meaningful relationships whilst retaining a professional distance. It's a very tricky balancing act, which I think they achieve with great aplomb, as indeed do print journalists such as the brilliant Michael Bailey.

Any football journalist will tell you about the barrages of negativity; readers or listeners are convinced you're biased or that you're in Delia/the manager/wee Paul McVeigh's pocket. I've heard all those comments before and, while I've toughened up a lot since the Man In The Stands cost me a tenner, it's tedious.

But that's not why I'm glad I'm no longer a football journalist. Nor is it the rise of the Citizen Journalist; I think it's brilliant that there is so much comment, so many ways for fans to get involved and vent their spleens than there was when I launched *FourFourTwo* a mind-boggling 22 years ago.

It's just that, although I've been called a member of the prawn sandwich brigade, nothing could be further from the truth. (For a start, I'm a vegetarian…!)

I'm an addict, an addict who doesn't want to have to clean up her act. Seriously. Football is a bonkers rollercoaster and I am now free to enjoy it for the dazzlingly brilliant spectacle that it is. I no longer have to try and make sense of it. I don't have to take it seriously any more. I have the luxury of immersing myself in the pantomime of the outrageously bad ref, wallowing in the dodgy decisions that never go our way, getting ridiculously angry about the many matches where we've been hard done by. I can swear about a player without feeling guilty because I know he's a really nice chap who's going through some bad personal stuff. I can collect bruises on my shins from leaping into the row in front of me celebrating a goal.

I don't have to be professional or answer to anyone. I can experience and express the highs and lows more freely. In short, I can have more fun.

Forgive me for illustrating my point with a story involving a Man United fan. When I was editor of *FourFourTwo* we ran a competition to win tickets to the FA Cup Final at Wembley. This guy, let's call him Dave, won one of them. The whole prize package must have been around five or six hundred quid. He got poshed up and came and sat with us in the Olympic Gallery. We had a nice three (four?) course lunch with complimentary wine and possibly champagne. Some ex-player came and talked to us over lunch. We got a free souvenir programme. We had more free drinks in a box somewhere. We had amazing seats at the front of the balcony. Neil Morrissey from *Men Behaving Badly* was sat behind us. It was mint.

But it was the one and only time I've felt sorry for a Manchester United fan. Dave squirmed in his seat, squirmed in his shiny new suit, tried to make small talk and eventually looked like he might attempt a stage dive into the seething mass of shouting, jumping Man U fans partying below us. I felt for him. I understood his pain, his discomfort at being at the party but not invited to dance. I watched as he clearly grappled with the idea of leaping down to be in amongst his people. And, being the caring soul that I am, I nearly gave him a helping hand…

Karen Buchanan invented, launched and edited *FourFourTwo* magazine before freelancing for national newspapers and magazines. She was a reporter, producer and presenter for BBC Radio Norfolk for several years and co-wrote Iwan Roberts' best selling diary of Norwich City's Championship-winning season, *All I Want For Christmas*. She is now a lecturer in creative media production at City College, Norwich.

7

Malcolm Robertson, now a familiar face on ITV Anglia, was Norwich City's first official press officer. He was working at Carrow Road at the height of turmoil over chairman Robert Chase, when Martin O'Neill came and went so quickly. Here he takes us behind the scenes of what we now know was a pivotal time for the club.

NIGHTMARE OF MY DREAM JOB

BY MALCOLM ROBERTSON

I was on the M6 near Birmingham when I got the call that convinced me my very brief career with Norwich City Football Club was effectively over.

It was December 1995 and I was the club's press officer, or so I thought. I'd had the job seven months, and although Norwich were in the second tier – supposedly only 'on loan to the Endsleigh League' – I was returning from Burnden Park, having witnessed Bryan Gunn's heroics as the Canaries knocked out Premier League Bolton Wanderers in a League Cup penalty shoot-out. It had been a welcome boost for a club that, to put it mildly, was in a bit of a state.

Paul Franklin was in charge of City that night. He had picked up the reins after Martin O'Neill had walked out on the club a few days earlier. I didn't know it, but the Bolton victory was to prove Paul's second and final game in charge. His Norwich managerial CV reads: P2 W1 L1.

The call that came was from Chris Wise, a sports writer at the *Eastern Daily Press*. He informed me that Norwich City chairman Robert Chase had just phoned, saying if the *EDP* was to speculate that Gary Megson will be returning to the club as the new manager, it wouldn't be wrong.

It seemed incredible that the club's press officer should be told about a hugely significant development at Carrow Road by a journalist. That seemed the wrong way around! I knew my days were numbered.

The job had started promisingly enough, with another call from the club. It was from Mike Souter, who was doing some public relations work for Robert Chase. Some of you may recognise Mr Souter's name.

One rather nosey colleague overheard my part of the conversation and asked what it was about. I said I'd been pretty much offered the press officer's job at Carrow Road.

'That's your dream job,' she said. I had to agree. Little did we know!

At the time, Norwich were doing quite nicely: not reaching the heights of the European adventure the previous season, but seemingly more than holding their own in the Premier League. Sadly, there was an astonishing collapse in the second half of the season, and I had the unenviable task of starting my new job in the May, the day after the Canaries had been relegated. Great timing!

Gary Megson had been briefly in caretaker charge but left as the Canaries went down. My opinion is that Chase wanted him to remain but for once had to bow to the wishes of vice chairman Jimmy Jones, who was pressing O'Neill's claims. The majority of fans were also demanding O'Neill be the new manager, so Chase – hardly Mr Popularity with supporters – reluctantly agreed.

To me – wearing both my employee and supporter hats – it was a brilliant appointment and if O'Neill had stayed the full season I'm convinced the Canaries would have been promoted. What followed, though, was a very public and highly damaging falling out between chairman and manager and although Chase initially survived O'Neill's departure, he was badly wounded.

I liked O'Neill. I'd always admired him as a player during his two stints with the Canaries. He came from Nottingham Forest late in the 1981-82 season and, with some inspiring performances, very nearly kept us up in the top tier that year.

John Bond took him briefly to Manchester City but the two didn't get on and in February 1982, O'Neill returned to Carrow Road with the Canaries well down the second tier table.

Again, he helped transform the team who won 14 out of their final 19 games to return to the top division at the first attempt. During that run, he played for Northern Ireland against England at Wembley on a Tuesday night and the next night was at Oakwell turning out for the Canaries in a crucial 1-0 win over Barnsley.

In the 1983-84 season, back at the top level, he played a key role in City ultimately comfortably retaining their status. It didn't look good with us bottom of the table going to Portman Road on Boxing Day, but O'Neill struck a magnificent 90th minute free kick from 25 yards to win the game 3-2. And another wonderful long-range strike in a 2-0 win at Liverpool later in the season very much justified manager Ken Brown's decision to entice the Northern Irishman back to Carrow Road.

Good players don't necessarily make good managers but O'Neill was one who did. O'Neill cut his managerial teeth at Wycombe Wanderers, taking them into the Football League for the first time. He was therefore a man in demand: ambitious, intelligent and articulate. Coming to Norwich seemed like a marriage made in heaven.

Initially, the relationship between Chase and O'Neill was civil, even cordial. I was given the task of arranging a press trip to Northern Ireland where the team was playing some pre-season matches. Both chairman and manager seemed in perfect harmony, talking optimistically about the forthcoming Football League campaign.

I was well aware the Press were looking for signs of tension between two forthright characters but at that stage there were none. Chase liked the fact O'Neill made his intentions clear from the start, sending home two players from that Irish trip for disciplinary reasons. I took some satisfaction from the fact that the media never got wind of that.

It was a rare moment of triumph for me in what was otherwise a horrible year.

Once O'Neill walked out, it felt like I was caught in the middle of a civil war. It was the year in which we had the appalling sight of police horses attempting to control angry supporters outside the main office at Carrow Road, as fans became increasingly furious about the actions of a chairman who had just lost O'Neill, the manager many thought might lead the club back to glory.

Where did it all go wrong? Well, O'Neill was never slow to voice his opinion and if that meant embarrassing the chairman, so be it. For his part, Chase wanted a manager who was less confrontational, more diplomatic. And when O'Neill's sometimes abrasive nature led to him making remarks to the referee during a defeat at Sheffield United, he earned an FA charge – all of which, Chase found unseemly.

It was all beginning to unravel and it was the Hull City player Dean Windass who finally pulled it apart. Windass became the most famous player Norwich City never had and nobody should underestimate the part he played, unwittingly, in what was the start of a very long, unhappy period in the club's playing fortunes.

O'Neill's belief was that although the City squad was poor, he thought it adequate enough to get promoted. If they could add Windass that might well seal it. Although he later made his name as a striker, at that stage he was playing in midfield, but he'd already demonstrated his eye for a goal.

Initial offers from Norwich were rebuffed, with Hull's chairman publicly critical of his Norwich counterpart over the way the bidding process was being handled. O'Neill added fuel to the fire by sarcastically claiming he wanted Windass before

the century was out and was angered by suggestions that one
of the directors didn't rate the player.

You can just imagine O'Neill's reaction. Directors exist to
play hosts to their counterparts from other clubs, not pass
judgement on footballers!

'O'Neill seeks showdown with Chase over Windass!'
screamed the *Eastern Evening News* headline. It was my unhappy
task to make the chairman aware of what the press were saying
and was then party to a vitriolic telephone exchange between
the chairman and manager, with Chase ominously threatening,
'If you want a showdown you'll get one.'

It was the beginning of the end. O'Neill's view was that a
director's poor opinion of Windass was just a smokescreen for
an altogether more serious issue: that Norwich were in a very
deep financial mess and simply couldn't afford him.

That claim appeared to have real substance, because six
months later Chase was pretty much stripped of his power
when youth development manager Gordon Bennett took on
the role of temporary chief executive to restructure the club's
debt and stave off bankruptcy.

I often wonder what might have been the outcome had
O'Neill stayed. Two days before the game at Leicester in
December 1995, he confided to me and club secretary Andrew
Neville that he would be leaving. We tried to dissuade him but
to no avail. He said he just couldn't work with Chase.

It was agreed that nobody from the club would be making
any comments about the situation before or in the immediate
aftermath of the game. I was confident that O'Neill's departure
would only become evident as the teams and officials took to
the field at Leicester's Filbert Street ground for a match being
shown live on Anglia TV.

I was surprised therefore when an Anglia producer called
me early on the morning of the game, seeking confirmation

that O'Neill had walked out on the club.

The game was up, although I advised Chase to say nothing that day and that any communication from the club should be via a statement.

Imagine my annoyance on being contacted by a journalist telling me the chairman had appeared on BBC Radio Norfolk talking about O'Neill's departure, saying the club was refusing to accept his resignation.

I know Souter was still advising Chase. Perhaps they chose to ignore my advice.

Like all fans, I've had some miserable trips home from away games over the years, but none more depressing than that day after the Leicester game, which City lost 3-2. O'Neill had gone and with him went the prospect of going up, despite us being close to the top of the table. A few days later, O'Neill was installed as Leicester's new manager, after Mark McGhee left the Foxes. To nobody's surprise O'Neill led them to promotion that season and on to a period of great success.

I got the distinct impression the chairman saw me as too close to O'Neill and he had little time for me after O'Neill's departure. His failure to inform me about Gary Megson coming back as the new manager seems to bear that out.

I'm often asked if I knew anything of the club's financial woes at the time. I don't think any of the employees did, even though O'Neill said he had his suspicions.

Chase was very accomplished at not giving anything away. I was often surprised by calls from journalists. One asked me why the club was now charging parents for their children to be Carrow Road ball boys and girls. You would have thought a press officer might just have been informed of this new policy, but no, this one was certainly taken aback by that call!

'Is this the meanest football club in England?' asked the *Daily Star* headline the next day. It was not the sort of PR I wanted for the club I'd supported so avidly since I was a boy.

The writing was on the wall for me and it hardly gave me much satisfaction that I survived slightly longer than Chase did.

It was on May 2, 1996, that he said goodbye and walked out of Carrow Road, selling his shares to former chairman Geoffrey Watling.

I followed a few days later; made redundant as new chief exec Bennett was forced into savage pruning to keep Norwich City afloat. That he was successful reflects huge credit on him, and all City fans owe Bennett a huge debt of gratitude.

Megson lasted a few weeks more before losing the role of Norwich manager for a second time. In came Mike Walker, for his second time in charge.

I'd a lot of time for Megson, a decent bloke unlucky to cop the flak flying around after O'Neill left. He was on a hiding to nothing and being forced to sell two of his prize assets, Jon Newsome and Ashley Ward, in a desperate attempt to balance the books, underlined the severity of the club's financial plight.

Like O'Neill before him, he was unaware of the extent of the crisis when he took the job.

I'd lost 'my dream job' but it had become a nightmare, made more distressing because this was my team and it was in a very bad way.

Perhaps I let my heart rule my head in taking on the role. It had given me a fascinating insight into the workings of a football club but I was also exposed to a very unedifying side of the game. It left a pretty bitter taste.

If it seems I've been critical of Robert Chase, then I should redress the balance by saying his foresight in buying land next to Carrow Road proved a very shrewd financial acquisition for the football club. They benefitted considerably from that after he left. He also oversaw Norwich City's highest league finish and first entry into Europe, but the fact they were relegated just two years later suggests history might judge him rather harshly.

For me, leaving was almost a happy release. It's not much fun being without a job with two young mouths to feed, but Carrow Road wasn't a very happy place when Gordon Bennett began to uncover the true extent of Norwich's financial woes.

Not once was my support for the team ever in question; a team my dad first took me to watch on September 29, 1962. That day was more famous for Tommy Bryceland's Norwich City debut than my introduction to Carrow Road but a 2-0 win over Derby County had me signed up to the Canaries for life. Bryceland – a highly skilled inside forward – remains one of my all-time favourites. He was the Wes Hoolahan of his day.

I'd first become aware of the Canaries during the famous 1959 FA Cup run. I can vaguely remember my father leaving for the semi-final replay with Luton Town at St Andrew's. An Aberdonian who had recently moved to Norfolk, he had no previous affinity to Norwich City but, like so many others, was swept along on a tide of euphoria as a third tier club knocked on Wembley's door.

I don't recall my father coming back, although he obviously did! I would have been asleep and not wanting to hear how City's great Wembley dream had died that day.

Those early years following the Canaries were pretty unspectacular. It seemed that every year they finished in the bottom half of tier two; the only real excitement was provided by a stunning win at League champions Manchester United – Best, Law and Charlton and all – in 1967.

It was the arrival of Ron Saunders two years later that took Norwich City to a new dimension. A further two years on, he guided the Canaries to the top division for the first time, and what great memories I have of supporting City in that memorable season.

The *coup de grâce* was applied in East London on April 24,

1972 as goals from Graham Paddon and Kenny Foggo confirmed City's elevation to the big time. Like excited schoolboys we fans ran onto Orient's Brisbane Road pitch in celebration of a magnificent achievement.

My pal Graham Robb's Mini ran out of petrol near Thetford on the way home – but that problem seemed worthwhile when the coach carrying the victorious players passed us on its way back to Norfolk.

Its failure to stop to offer help was forgotten by the time we were refuelled and on our way to Watford on the following Saturday to see Dave Stringer score the goal that clinched the second tier title. How fitting that a Norfolk man and one of the club's greatest ever players should be the one to do it.

In those days before local radio and long before social media, the only way of getting an immediate and thorough analysis of a Norwich City match was by buying the local classified results newspaper, *The Pink Un*. There was the weekly ritual of queuing outside the newsagents in Sheringham, waiting for it to arrive. If City had won the excitement was all the greater, and if you'd scored in a local football game the previous weekend and your name might just have made it on to page seven, the cigars would be out that night!

The Pink Un in that format was a great institution and I'm sure it is sadly missed by many older supporters. It supplied that wonderful 'Bly Bly Babes' headline after Terry Bly's two goals dumped Manchester United's Busby babes out of the FA Cup in 1959. And in my time of reading it, there was 'Hot Cross Bone Day' after David Cross and Jimmy Bone scored in a 2-0 win at Charlton Athletic on Easter Saturday in 1972. Pure genius.

My affection for the *The Pink Un* is because I was later lucky enough to work on it. Employed as a young journalist on the *Eastern Daily Press*, I was offered the chance to cover Norwich

City's fortunes in 1978. I have to be thankful to a certain Mick Dennis who relinquished the post for a job in London and subsequent career on various national newspapers. Mick was a hard act to follow. I expect he'll leave that bit in!

I must admit, too, that I had considerable trepidation about having to try and separate my role as a reporter from that of a fan of the club.

I well remember my *Pink Un* debut: September 26, 1978 at Coventry City's Highfield Road. It's probably best described as an inauspicious start. Nerves clearly got the better of me because I forgot the old adage that less is more.

In those days you hired a telephone from a local press agency and once you'd established contact with the Norwich office and hopefully a clear line, you provided a running commentary of the game for a copy-taker on a typewriter back in Norwich.

I was fortunate enough to have a delightful retired gentleman by the name of Ralph Potter to take down my supposed words of wisdom. Ralph was incredibly quick at typing and needed to be that day because I was unstoppable. He had a nice way with words and suggested I was being slightly 'verbose'. Less sensitive was sub-editor Peter March, a Cockney who could always be relied on for a more forthright approach.

'For God's sake Robbo! You're not writing a bloody novel,' he bellowed down the phone.

To complete my less than perfect day, Norwich lost 4-1. A lot of lessons were learned – not least that you had to have a very thick skin to cope with Marchy!

There was never a dull moment covering the fortunes of Norwich City in those days. That's because John Bond was at the helm. He'd taken over from Ron Saunders in 1973 and although unable to save the Canaries from relegation that season, brought them back to the top division at the first attempt. Signing players like Martin Peters, Ted MacDougall,

Phil Boyer and Kevin Reeves, Bond brought a real sense of excitement to Carrow Road and if ever a style of football matched the personality of the manager, that was it.

From a journalist's point of view, Bond was a joy to work with. He was an extravagant character, courted by the media. Although, from my local perspective, I was always concerned that a good quote and story I'd missed might appear in a national newspaper.

Having said that, Bondy was always very good to the local reporters. He allowed us to travel on the team bus, which was a great way of getting to know the players. And – amazingly when you consider this now – he let us sit in on his team talks at away games.

These were delivered at the hotel just before the players left for the game. They provided a fascinating insight into the sort of thinking and detailed preparation that a top coach put into analysing the opposition, detecting their strengths and weaknesses. It didn't always work. I can recall quite a complex way of trying to cope with Ian Rush and Kenny Dalglish in a game at Anfield. Liverpool won 6-0 and Bond's tactical plan was in tatters. But for Kevin Keelan, it could have been ten.

On the plane home, City centre-half Phil Hoadley urged me not to be too harsh on the players. And, with total honesty, I wrote that you could have had the best defenders in the world playing that day and Rush and Dalglish would still have run amok.

Bond was good company and always entertaining. You were invariably invited to his hotel room the night before a match along with coaching staff Ken Brown and John Sainty. The drinks flowed and so did the football chat. The unwritten rule was what was said was not to be reported but you got an idea which players the club might be interested in signing. The only problem was, having consumed a fair few glasses you'd completely forgotten those names by the next morning!

Inevitably I had my favourites as players: not necessarily through their ability but because they were happy to spend time with me on often long away trips.

Hoadley was one of them. Mick McGuire was another. I liked him as a player and he was a thoroughly nice bloke. Greg Downs was always entertaining and did a very good impression of John Bond, obviously out of sight and hearing of the manager!

O'Neill was another good guy and always very interesting to listen to. The vast majority of players never surfaced for breakfast but O'Neill usually did. He had an opinion on most things and it emerged he would often visit courtrooms around the country and sit in on high-profile murder cases. He'd been a law student but instead opted for a career in football.

Not all the players were comfortable with having the local media in their midst. Tony Powell would often greet me with the words 'poison pen' and Graham Paddon questioned how a journalist could give opinions on a game when they'd never played it to any level. I was thankful that Joe Royle provided the answer I was struggling to come up with – telling Paddon that a male gynaecologist never had a baby but could be trusted to do his job. I'm not sure Paddon was convinced.

Despite his later Ipswich Town connections, Royle was another I had a lot of time for. I can well recall the coach trip back from Liverpool after he'd scored in a 2-0 win at his former club Everton, whose fans gave him a standing ovation after the goal.

On the way home we stopped at Bedford for fish and chips. It was full of Ipswich fans in fairly sombre mood after losing to Manchester City in the FA Cup semi-final at Villa Park.

As the bus pulled away, Justin Fashanu decided it was time for a bit of 'mooning' aimed at our friends from Suffolk. Cue much laughter from the rest of the coach before Royle realised the possible repercussions of the incident, insisting to all and sundry that none of us had seen what happened. His remarks were clearly directed at myself and *Eastern Evening News* football reporter Bill Walker, and of course nothing was reported in the local press.

I worried that an Ipswich fan witnessing the offending gesture might contact a national newspaper but happily the story never saw the light of day.

That was typical Fashanu, full of mischief and fun. He was a very likeable lad and whenever I was contacted by someone asking if I could get a player to do a charity event, Justin would always oblige and never asked for a penny. He was a good-hearted soul, shrewd enough to realise the value of positive PR. His untimely death in 1998 was an awful tragedy.

Jimmy Neighbour was another Norwich player around that time who is sadly no longer with us. He was the reason behind a big falling out between John Bond and me in April 1979 when Norwich were playing Manchester United at Carrow Road.

City had been two-up but were pegged back to 2-2 and the equalising goal had its origins from a slack pass from Neighbour on the edge of the United penalty area, athough one could only admire the speed of the United break and subsequent finish.

Never one to hold back in a press conference, Bond described Neighbour's performance as 'disgraceful.' I thought that was a bit harsh and said as much in my Monday match report, wondering whether that comment might have been better left in the dressing room.

I got a call at home from my sports editor Peter Ware, saying Bond was furious with me and that I had no business voicing an opinion on his remarks. I was to be banned from the Trowse training ground and from covering games at Carrow Road, although the club relented and allowed me to take my seat in the press box but not at post-match press conferences.

Although disappointed with Bond, I was more annoyed with my bosses at the *EDP*. They gave me the impression they weren't prepared to be dictated to by Carrow Road, but in the end did nothing and left me to stew. In those days, local newspapers were the only means of receiving comprehensive coverage of Norwich City and I felt that if the paper spelled out to its readers what had happened and why there was to be no coverage of anything related to the Canaries, the club might have had second thoughts – bearing in mind all our reports and stories were effective publicity for matches.

Neighbour asked to meet me in the Mustard Pot, one of the closest pubs to Carrow Road. There was no need for him to apologise for inadvertently landing me in trouble, but he very kindly did. We had a good laugh about it afterwards and he was always very obliging in being a radio pundit at Norwich matches in London when I later moved to BBC Radio Norfolk.

Bond and I buried the hatchet during the close season. Our relationship was never quite the same again and I was disappointed to read in a national paper that goalkeeper Roger Hansbury was to miss the start of the next season because of a broken leg sustained in training. The manager hadn't mentioned that to me when I phoned him about any updates at the club.

Bond left for Manchester City during that season, to be replaced at Carrow Road by Ken Brown: a lovely man. I was delighted for Brown that he led the Canaries to their Milk Cup triumph at Wembley in 1985, which would have meant European football but for the ban imposed on English clubs that same season, following the Heysel Stadium tragedy in Brussels.

It was during Brown's reign at Norwich that I decided to call time on travelling with the team to away matches and instead make my own way. It had been a very cosy arrangement but there had been one occasion where I felt my journalistic integrity could be called into question.

It was the first day of the 1981-82 season when newly-relegated Norwich met newly-promoted Rotherham United at Millmoor. City were a shambles and lost 4-1 to Emlyn Hughes' team. On the journey back after a couple of drinks and discussion with players and management, I'd almost convinced myself the Canaries had been unlucky.

They weren't and I realised the time had come to be more independent. Although you desperately want the team to do well, you're a reporter as well as a supporter and you have to be true to your instincts.

There's an awful lot to be said for being close to the players, though, not least the chance of ready quotes and a lift home after a long away trip. My colleague Bill Walker wasn't particularly happy with my decision but I was comfortable with it.

By the time Brown was sacked by Robert Chase in 1987, I was working at Radio Norfolk. Enter David Stringer to the Carrow Road hot seat. Dave's place in Norwich City folklore was already assured and I just hoped that reputation wouldn't be sullied by an ill-judged foray into football management.

There were to be no fears on that score. Stringer proved a very successful manager and like Bond and Brown before him was great to work with. One of my fondest memories followed the 'Battle of Highbury' in November 1989 when Arsenal beat Norwich 4-3. Virtually every player on the field was involved in a brawl after the Gunners scored their winning goal. Even allowing for my view of events having been possibly coloured by green and yellow spectacles, the Canaries did seem to be on the wrong end of some questionable refereeing decisions.

Despite the prospect of an FA charge for the rucus, Stringer commendably fronted-up to talk to me afterwards. He insisted we found a quiet corner of Highbury so his comments couldn't be overheard by national reporters. He'd earlier declined to speak to the written media. Radio Norfolk had an exclusive interview and Stringer had again shown himself to be a top man in my book.

Some of my favourite memories are of Stringer and Duncan Forbes together. Everyone knows what a good defensive partnership they had but they were quite a double act off the pitch as well. Stringer was invariably the butt of Forbes's jokes; the insinuation being that he was tight with money. 'Stringer's just been arrested,' he told me, 'for breaking into his wallet. But the police let him off because it was his first offence!'

After his playing days, Forbes became the club's supporters' liaison officer and was responsible for arranging travel to away games. In 1982, he chartered a train to an FA Cup third round match at Stoke City, won 1-0 by the Canaries. We were with him and as the train pulled out of Stoke station, a brick was thrown through one of the windows. Having checked everyone was okay, Forbes said in that rich Scottish burr of his, 'It's a shame Stringer wasn't on board. He would have headed it back!'

When Forbes and Stringer were in tandem, you were always guaranteed plenty of fun and laughter.

These days, my only involvement with the club is as a season ticket holder. Although it's a matter of some regret that my son chooses to support England rather than Scotland, I'm delighted he's inherited his father's love of the Canaries – and in no way was put off by the fact that two of his first away games were 6-1 and 5-0 defeats at Port Vale and Ipswich respectively.

Seeing his pride and joy in that wonderful play-off final win at Wembley in May 2015 was something I will always cherish. He's seen for himself the ups and downs associated with supporting Norwich City: in my humble and unashamedly slightly biased opinion, the best football club in the world!

Malcolm Robertson was the Norwich City correspondent of the *Eastern Daily Press* before joining BBC Radio Norfolk. He worked as press officer for Norwich City and is now a reporter for ITV Anglia.

8

Adam Drury is the one that nearly got away.

He was at Norwich as a schoolboy but left to join Peterborough. Eight years later, manager Nigel Worthington bought him back.

He wore the Canaries' yellow for 11 years (and seven more managers), and saw it all: the rise, decline and rise again of the club. If, as cliché insists, football can be a rollercoaster, then he was at the club for the entire ride.

This is his self-critical account of that adventure.

GOING UP, DOWN, UP

BY ADAM DRURY

Someone told me that I am the only player who was at Norwich before the 2002 play-off final, in the team who won the Football League in 2004, was with the club as we went from the Premier League right down to League One and then was still a Norwich player through all the climb back up to the Premier League again. So my 11 years were certainly not dull.

The absolute low point is not hard to guess. I was in the team that lost 7-1 to Colchester at Carrow Road on the first day of the season in League One. Fortunately for me, when Paul Lambert took over as manager soon afterwards, he didn't remember I was on the pitch that day! But I was.

The next day I went to the Tesco near where I lived in Hethersett to get milk or something. A guy, quite old, parked his car, got out, walked past me, looked at me, and said, 'Surprised you're showing your face after yesterday.' I just let it go. He'd got a point.

But before that 2009-10 season, I'd had the chance to move. A few clubs were asking about me, but I was like, 'Don't be silly, I don't want to leave here.' I could have got a few more quid going somewhere else but I didn't want to move. I just thought Norwich was the right club for me.

In fact, I don't know how many supporters realise that I was with Norwich as a schoolboy before I played for Peterborough. I don't think Norwich fans know that that club down the road in Suffolk were interested in me when I was at Peterborough.

But they do know that I chose Norwich.

I grew up in Cottenham, just north of Cambridge. Mum had been an air hostess and dad was a tiler. He still is. When I was at primary school I was playing for my village team and got selected for the county. I played a few games in Norwich and was invited to their Centre of Excellence. But because I lived in Cambridgeshire, I had to go to the Centre of Excellence that Norwich ran in Hitchin.

My brother, who is a couple of years younger than me, was going there as well. He was a left-winger, taller than me then and now, and a lot better technically than me. I think he could have gone a long way in the game, but football just wasn't his passion. He had lots of other interests and liked to go out with friends, so at 16 or 17 he decided he didn't want to take football as seriously as I did.

I understand that. It was quite difficult having mates if you were spending all your spare time trying to be a professional footballer. In holidays, instead of doing school trips or just hanging about with friends, I was spending 23 hours on a ferry for Centre of Excellence trips to places like Denmark.

When you go back to school after the holiday, your schoolmates can be harsh. In the playground they would assume, because I'd been away on a football trip, that I was a bighead. That's why my best friend was and is someone who'd been on those football trips with me: Niall Inman, who was in the Republic of Ireland team that finished third in the world under-20 championships in 1997. He played for quite a few clubs. After leaving Peterborough, his longest stint was at Kettering Town.

Don't get me wrong. I'm not saying, 'Oh, it was terrible being a young footballer'. It was definitely what I wanted to do. But when I got to 13, it seemed like all the lads at the Norwich Centre of Excellence were getting schoolboy forms and I wasn't offered one. I was thinking, 'What's going on here?'

Kit Carson, who had been in charge of the Norwich youth set-up, had gone to Peterborough and I knew he would have me, so I asked to talk to the Norwich people: Gordon Bennett (who was head of the youth system), Keith Webb (youth team manager), and Sammy Morgan and Mike Sutton, who were the coaches of my year group. I went and asked about my chances of schoolboy forms.

I got a letter saying, 'Thanks for your time'. So that was it. I went to Peterborough where I did get schoolboy forms and then a youth training scheme (YTS) place. My best friend Niall and I lived with the same family and then, at the end of my YTS, we both got year-to-year pro deals.

It was while I was on the YTS scheme that I met my wife, Helen. Over the years she has had some tough health issues to deal with in her family but she has always supported me through my less serious ups and downs.

I thought there was going to be a down in the summer just before I turned 18 when there was a news flash. 'Breaking news: Barry Fry has bought Peterborough!' He was famous for a huge turnover of players and I thought I'd be out of the door. But he said he would give me a chance and he was as good as his word.

I made my debut the following May and went on to play 150 games, win their player of the season award and appear in the play-off final at the old Wembley when they won promotion from the fourth tier. That was in 2000. I was 21. I got kicked in the head in the first half and came off with concussion.

Near the end of the following season, in the March, we were on the bus on the way to an away game and Baz – which was what everyone called Barry Fry – said, 'Norwich have been in for you'.

Peterborough were in the third tier and Norwich were in the second. Norwich didn't have anyone who was playing consistently at left back. I thought it was a good move and the deal went through on transfer deadline day, 2001. That's the only time my name has ever been involved in any news flashes.

My new manager was Nigel Worthington and I soon got nicknamed 'Son of Nigel' because he'd been a left back, stuck me straight in the team and more or less kept me there. The Norwich lads reckoned I had to be a relative!

My first game was against Grimsby at Carrow Road. The lads were like, 'This is a massive six-pointer. If we don't win this we'll be favourites to get relegated'. I said, 'What?!' I'd only just signed, and was so happy to be at Norwich. But they'd lost four games on the spin and were sliding down the table. If we went down, I'd be back in the same division as Peterborough. But we won 2-1 and got on a bit of roll to the end of the season, and it continued the next season.

I couldn't have been happier. I was 22 when I joined Norwich and turned 23 just before the next season, 2001-02. I was in a team with good players. There were men like Craig Fleming, Malky Mackay, who was just establishing himself, Phil Mulryne in midfield, Rob Green in goal. Up front there was Iwan Roberts and we had Paul McVeigh. I don't think everyone gives Paul the credit for how influential he was, particularly in that 2001-02 season. People perhaps forget the goals he chipped in. He was never going to race away from anyone but he was technically good and a thinker about the game. He will tell you that he set up most of my goals, and I wouldn't argue. But scoring was never my forte.

I was a defender: a left back. I would always back myself, defensively, in a one versus one. If you want to take me on, I will back myself to stop you going past me with the ball. And if your job is to get the ball into the middle for your top scorer, well, I'm going to prevent that.

It was a Peterborough youth team coach called Jim Walker who converted me from a winger or central midfielder to left

back and then there was another guy at Peterborough, Chris
Turner, who was massive on just defending. He took me daily
for one-versus-one sessions. I was already quite good at it, but
he drilled me and drilled me, and made me a better tackler. He'd
say, 'You don't get beat. You don't get beat'.

I wasn't overly quick but I concentrated well, and I learned
to read the game, to read what an opponent was doing. I had a
good ability to change direction quickly.

The modern game has changed. Defending isn't the main
thing for full backs and you hear people say, 'He's a good left
back but he can't defend'. In my book that means he isn't a
good left back.

Being able to defend at full back was more important then,
though, probably because everyone played 4-4-2 and you'd
be up against an out-and-out winger every week. If he went
past you, your team was in trouble, but not many got past me.
Throughout my career I could say that. I'm my own biggest
critic and there were things about my game I wasn't happy with,
but that wasn't one of them.

Our manager – whether it was Nigel Worthington, Paul
Lambert, whoever – would say, 'If you stop your man getting
the ball over, we stop them scoring'. So I would think, 'Right,
I can play a big part in winning this game'. Perhaps the media
and even the fans didn't always see that, but I wasn't after headlines. I wanted to do the job the manager, and my team-mates,
understood was important. No matter who you put me against,
I'd think, 'He won't get round me.' I played against Gareth Bale
and Cristiano Ronaldo and thought the same. I just regarded
it as my personal challenge. Mind you, when we played Southampton once and Bale was left back, getting the ball from the
keeper and running the length of the pitch, I was like, 'Please
don't switch wings!'

In that 2001-02 season, my first full season as a Norwich

player, we reached the play-off final at Cardiff for promotion to the Premier League. The two semi-final matches against Wolves were fantastic, unreal. Those were the times when I said to myself, 'This is why you wanted to be a pro. This is the reason you pushed yourself. These are the games you want'.

Up the spine of that team we had lads who all played more than 40 games that season: Greeny, Malky, Flem, Gary Holt. Then several had played nearly 40: me, Mulryne and McVeigh. It was a settled team and we'd all got there together. At Wolves that night for the second leg of the semi-final, we just weren't going to throw away all we'd worked for. We'd won the first leg 3-1 at home and at Molineux we held out for 77 minutes before they scored. And then we kept them out until the end and went through 3-2.

As for the final against Birmingham, well, because I'd had concussion and come off in the 2000 final with Peterborough, I didn't really feel like I was a full part of the occasion. So to get to another final two years later, even though it was Cardiff and not Wembley, was just brilliant. When we walked out before the game, with the stadium roof closed and one half of the ground blue and the other yellow and green, again, I thought, 'This is what it is all about'.

Iwan scored in extra-time and thought it was Golden Goal and that he's won it. He went racing off and I was like, 'Where's he going?' Then they equalised and it went to penalties. The lads who missed ours, Mulryne and Daryl Sutch, well, you'd have backed them to put them away. Mullers always placed the ball so well, but on the day, instead of side-footing it, tried to blast it. Sutchy had never missed a penalty ever in training but he rolled his one wide. But I can't talk because I think Greeny would have been in front of me in the line to take one.

I thought, 'I had concussion when Peterborough won. Now I've played a full game for Norwich but we've lost on penalties.

That might be it. I might not get another chance of winning something'. But it turned out there was a lot more to come.

The following season, 2002-03, we had a bit of a reaction to losing the final, I think, and didn't do so well. But I won the fans' player of the season award, which I was very, very proud of.

Then, at the start of the next season, Nigel made me captain. I couldn't believe it. I'm not a shouter on the field – nor off it, either. I am just Adam: just happy to do my job and go home. Away from football I keep myself to myself. I am one of those that, if there is a night out, I wouldn't be noticed much. I certainly wouldn't be the centre of attention.

So becoming captain was a strange one. I remember we were out on the main pitch at Colney and Nigel said, 'Adam, I am thinking about making you captain. What do you think?' I told him I was honoured, and that it was unexpected. Then I said, 'I want to ask one or two of the other lads what they think about it.'

There were big characters at the club, like Malky, Iwan and Flem. So I said, 'I want to check with them. I don't want to upset the dressing room and I am not vocal like some of the others'. Nigel said, 'That's fine. They give leadership. That's the way they are and the way they play. But I want you because of the way you conduct yourself'.

I did go and ask Malky, Iwan and Flem and every single one of them was brilliant. Of course they had some fun. They said, 'Well, you're Son of Nigel, so of course you should be captain'. I explained to them that I hadn't asked for the job and they all said, 'No problem'. That meant everything to me. Without them backing me like that I would have found it difficult to go to someone like Iwan, who was an absolute icon, and say anything that might have been stepping on his toes.

The way that 2003-04 season turned out – winning the

championship, the open-top bus tour, holding the trophy up on the balcony of City Hall and so on – I am so glad now that Nigel asked me, that the lads backed me, and that I took on the job. I wouldn't change what happened.

But I do think that I tried to play up to being a captain, rather than just being myself, maybe. I was so busy trying to make sure I was being captain that it took away a little from my game. Knowing what I do now, if I could go back, I would still take the job. But would I do it slightly differently? Maybe.

I felt I had a dip in form when we reached the Premier League. Defensively I didn't have any problems. On the ball, though, I thought I could have done better. If I'd believed in myself a bit more I'd have been okay. But I got it into my head that perhaps I was giving the ball away too much. I probably wasn't but I over-analysed and the team was losing, not doing great, and I was picking holes in my own game.

I wasn't fazed by the players I was facing. There were some pretty decent ones, but that wasn't my problem. I just felt I could do more, contribute more to a team that wasn't getting enough points.

I was still doing my job defensively, I believe. I was proud and satisfied to be a consistent performer at that job: a regular seven or eight out of ten player. But you do get stereotyped a bit and my label was, 'Good one-v-one defender. Could be a bit better on the ball'. And I believed that. Now, at the age I've reached, I look at the games and think, 'You know what, you weren't bad on the ball either – but you didn't have enough belief in that bit of the game'.

Anyway, we had Darren Huckerby to do the stuff at the other end of the pitch. He'd joined us in the season we won the Championship and was the opposite to me. With me, if some-one ran at me, it was a matter of pride that he wouldn't get past me. With Hucks, if he took the ball up to a defender, we'd all back him to take it past the opposition player.

In training, Hucks and I never really faced each other. I think he was scared of me! We didn't see much of each other on a Saturday either, because he was always up the other end of the field attacking and leaving the defensive duties to me.

Actually, we wanted Hucks up the opposition end, because if we could get the ball to him, he'd do some damage. And the other team had to leave one or two men to mark him. So, although I joked about him not tracking back, Hucks made my job easier, because opponents on my side of the pitch were always chasing him and not bothering me!

I had a really good understanding with Hucks. He'd say, 'Don't bang the ball over the top. Drop it in front of me'. So I'd drop it in so that he'd take it on the bounce with his back to the defender, the defender would close him down and Hucks would spin and be away. And I'd watch him from the halfway line thinking, 'Go on Hucks, take them all on!'

I had a good arrangement with old 'Three Lungs', Gary Holt, too. I could stop a winger going down the line but if he liked to check inside, it could be more tricky, and that was when Gary was absolutely brilliant. He'd always be there. So, if someone did try to check inside they'd run straight into Holty. Trust me, you don't want to do that! I'd say to him, 'Gary if your man is giving you a difficult time, make him pass out to my winger and I'll take care of things.' The little understandings we had in that team were outstanding.

The 2004-05 season in the Premier League was an unforgettable experience. I was captain, so I remember walking out at Arsenal, and I'm next to Patrick Vieira. At Man United I walked out with Roy Keane. At Tottenham it was Jamie Redknapp. At Liverpool it was Steven Gerrard. But I wasn't intimidated. I was like, 'Wow, this isn't bad.'

At Old Trafford I had the ball in the corner and Keane came

across and smashed me in half. The whole of Old Trafford was chanting, 'Kea-no, Kea-no', and I was just a crumpled heap. But I still just thought, 'This is the top, top league'. I was sort of thinking, 'There are so many players, decent players, who never get to be cut in half by Roy Keane!'

Another game that stands out, and not for a good reason, was the second match of the season, against Arsenal. Lauren should have been sent off for bringing down Hucks but we ended up losing 4-1. They were The Invincibles, though, and Thierry Henry was doing that thing where he knocks the ball past you and actually runs off the pitch as he goes around you after it. He was giving people head starts and just gliding past. Not on my side though!

I remember the ball pinged around our box and it came to me. They'd been playing total football and when the ball came to me, on the penalty spot, I thought, 'I'll play us out of trouble here.' I took a touch, Freddie Ljungberg nicked the ball off my toes and Robert Pires got their third goal.

We were against the elite, probably the best players in the world at that time, and it was an eye-opener. But at the same time I was like, 'This is where I want to be competing.'

Our problem, until we signed Dean Ashton in January, was that we didn't have goals. Once Deano was in the team, we got going and we gave ourselves a chance of staying up. So the less said about the game at Fulham, on the last day of that season, the better – except that we had to win and so when we went one-down after ten minutes, we chased it and for them it became party time. In case you don't know, they won 6-0. I certainly don't need reminding.

That summer I was gutted and when the new season started, we'd go to Championship grounds and look around before the game and think, 'We've got to do all this all over again.' The games come two a week, it's a grind, and you are thinking, 'We worked so hard to get out of this once but now here we are again.' There was definitely a reaction to relegation that was hard to shake off.

It's Saturday, Tuesday, Saturday. You are never going to be 100 per cent fit. You are going to have knocks and niggles, but that is when you need people who you can bank on week-in and week-out. I think that is when being a left back who is a seven or an eight every game is not a bad thing.

We were favourites to go straight back up, but we never got going and then a decline set in and it ended, eventually, with Nigel leaving. Next there was the spell in which we had different managers and instead of challenging for promotion, we were fighting to stay in the Championship.

In the September of the 2007-08 season, I did my knee and missed a year. The injury happened just before Glenn Roeder came in, during the three games or so Jim Duffy was in charge. The first diagnosis was a calf strain but, after having treatment for a while, I could feel my knee pushing out to the side as I walked. Hucks said to me, 'Well both your knees push out to the side. They always have'.

I had it checked by a top guy in Nottingham. I sat in the room with him and he said, 'Yeah, you won't play again this season.' Basically the thing that joins my hamstring to the knee had snapped. I admit I had tears in my eyes because I wasn't expecting that at all.

As a manager, Glenn did bring in some good players – Wes Hoolahan and Sammy Clingan for instance. But he brought in so many lads on loan that we weren't allowed to have them all in the team. Glenn was trying to raise the quality quickly, and if you bring in one or two, like we did with Hucks and Peter Crouch under Nigel, that's great. But you can't have the whole group made up of people on loan who've got no real investment in results. Some of the loan lads were thinking, 'If

I have a bad game it's not the end of the world because in a month I'm going back to my own club'.

Glenn's way worked for the season he joined us, 2007-08, though. He kept us up when it had looked a pretty bad situation when he arrived in the October. And results were still bad for most of the season. I remember talking to Hucks after one defeat, just after Christmas. He rang me from the bus on the way back and that was the lowest I'd ever heard him. And it was hard for me, even though I was injured.

Eventually, during the 2008-09 season, I was almost ready to play again – until my hamstring snapped during a training session. That was a low-point. So Dave Carolan (the sports scientist), Neal Reynolds and Pete Shaw (the physios) all deserve special thanks. A long-lay off can be a lonely business, but they helped me immensely with all the rehab work day after day and, in the end, they got me back playing again.

But the results in that 2008-09 season were terrible and Glenn lost his job. Bryan Gunn took over in the January, but we went down to the third tier: exactly where I'd been when I left Peterborough. Relegation was a massive disappointment. Massive, no question.

Then we had that shocking start to the 2009-10 season against Colchester and their manager, Paul Lambert, took over. Once he came in and set us up with a diamond in midfield, we started tearing teams apart. It was a system that got Wes on the ball, and we had another Holty – Grant – to score goals and it just went from there.

In the October, we had Carlisle away and my wife was due to go into labour with our daughter, Isla. I was thinking, 'Please start labour before we start the six-hour journey'. And she did. She went into labour on the Friday and Paul let me stay behind.

But when I came out of the hospital at one in the morning, after being with my wife at the birth, I'd got a 121 message. It was the manager. 'Adam, it's Paul Lambert, give us a call.'

He told me I had to be at Norwich airport for 10 o'clock to fly up to the game with Delia Smith, Michael Wynn Jones, David McNally and some of the other directors. I was like, 'Really!?'. But he was like, 'Yep. You're playing, so make sure you prepare properly'.

So I flew up there. We landed in what looked like just an ordinary field, and went to the ground. Wes didn't have his shin pads so he put a programme down each sock. The lads were giving me stick about having it cushy on the flight up when they'd been stuck on a coach but Wes scored, we won 1-0 and Paul let me fly back to be with my wife. I waved to all the others and said, 'See you later.' I was back in Norwich in 40 minutes.

I know we were in League One, but winning that division was still winning a proper competition, a proper trophy. It felt good to be around the club again, and I'd played a full season again. I wasn't stupid, though. I knew I was getting older, and when the manager brought Marc Tierney in from his old club, Colchester, for the Championship season, I knew I was no longer automatic first choice. Every transfer window I'd been like, 'Have we been linked with a left back?' Well, now we'd bought one. So I thought, 'Right, I've got to raise my game'.

I got on well with 'T'. He did better cartwheels than me, I know, and was definitely more of a madman, but because we played in the same position we did a lot of training together. We'd be standing at the same cone waiting our turns to do some drill, and we got chatting, so I became friends with the man who was trying to take my place.

The manager had a way with lads who weren't playing of keeping them on-side, which is one of the toughest bits of man-management. But I did get games. I played in 22 in that 2010-11 Championship campaign and, again, we had a feeling. It was like, 'We can do something this season'. And we did. Up we went, back to the Premier League.

I turned 33 that summer. The manager would have been within his rights to have said, 'You're in a position where pace is important. See you later.' But he didn't. He gave me another year and I played 16 games, was in the team that won at Tottenham, and played a part in finishing 12th.

That season meant I qualified for a testimonial, so in May 2012 a Norwich team with a few guests beat Celtic, who were Scottish champions at Carrow Road. Happy days.

The gaffer came to me, though, and said, 'Look, you're 34. You can stay and do some coaching, but you're not going to get many games.' But everyone you speak to says keep playing as long as you can and I wanted to play as often as I could in the last few years.

So I am with all the lads on a trip to Vegas to celebrate a great season. I get back to the room I am sharing with David Fox. The phone goes. It's Neil Warnock.

I went to Leeds, had two years, but it didn't turn out to be a big Vegas win. I wasn't Warnock's type of player. He wanted me to scalp the ball up the field and the player with it. That wasn't me and so I didn't get picked. I moved the family up there, two kids and the missus, because I wanted to do it properly, but it didn't happen for me. Towards the end of my time at Leeds I was driving to Cambridge on a midweek evening to play with my old mates. I just wanted to play.

Then I went to Bradford in the third tier on loan, and did okay. I definitely wasn't as quick as I had been, but in that league nobody got past me. But they signed a young lad and I knew I'd got to make a decision.

Nobody came in for me so, in September 2014, a month after my 36th birthday, I said to my wife, 'Look, I haven't a clue what I am going to do next, but that's it.' I was more than happy with what I'd done in my career. I hope most people would say

I'd always done my best.

I look back and I think it was a privilege and a thrill to play with guys like Wes and Hucks. They were the two I would pick out as game-changers. Hucks had so much sheer ability and pace. With Wes there were times in training when you knew what he was going to do – all those left-footed tricks with the ball – but you just couldn't stop him.

Hucks was one of the best trainers too. But Wes? Well I remember in Scotland with Gunny before the start of the League One season that Wes missed a morning session because he'd got a tight hamstring. He was all right for the afternoon five-a-sides though. Grant Holt was another who was better at playing than training. I remember me, him and our two wives went to the BBC sports awards in London with Jake Humphries and we got back to Norfolk at some stupid time. Next day, for the only time in my career, I spent the whole training session hiding. But Holty sort of over-compensated and was chasing everywhere, really giving it some effort. I said to him, 'You need to go out more often'. But he was terrible again on the Friday. And brilliant in the game on the Saturday, of course.

I am very privileged to have made good friends through football like both Holts (even though they both love a moan!) and David Fox (a key player in our diamond formation under Paul Lambert and great golfing buddy!). Being close friends with Hucks helped our understanding on the pitch, I think.

I was lucky as well to have a good bond with the fans. It is not often that a left back wins support like I received (especially a non-scoring left back!). It was an honour that I treasure.

Who was the hardest player in any of the Norwich teams I played in? Well, we had a few I was glad were on my side, but you might be surprised by the man I'd say was the one I'd least like on the other side: Youssef Safri. In a 50-50, he would do you, and not necessarily legally.

You have these memories, and over the years you get to know people like Delia and her mum, Etty. They loved my son Ethan, who was my first-born. Even now if I bring him to a game they love to see him.

That comes from staying for so long. I am lucky to have those long relationships and memories, good and bad; that link. That's why when there is a good time at the club – when the team is winning and there is a feel-good thing around the place – you are just so happy for all the people at the club.

One of the people I've known all the time I've been at Norwich is Ian Thornton, chief executive of the club's Community Sports Foundation. Shortly after I stopped playing, he phoned me. He knew I was bored and needed some direction in my life. He knew I didn't want hand-outs or want the club to give me some sort of role just because I'd been a player for 11 years.

So Ian rang me up and talked me into trying coaching. When this book comes out, I shall be coaching an under-18 shadow squad with lads who don't get taken on by the academy. They'll do a BTEC course, so they'll get qualifications and might go to Lowestoft or somewhere like that to play – or they might be a late developer and turn out to be a Jamie Vardy. I'll let you know if I find one of those.

I'm finding some of it challenging, but that's a good thing, and it gives me a continuing, proper role at the club that has been my life. Plus, I can go to Tesco on a Sunday morning without too much worry.

Adam Drury was a Norwich player for 11 years and made more than 300 appearances. He was player of the season in 2001-02 and captain when City won the Football League in 2004. As the club plunged to its lowest ebb for half a century, relegation to the third tier, he refused moves away – and remained a City man as the club climbed back to the Premier League. He is **a** Hall of Fame member.

9

The start was sensational for talented teenager **Darren Eadie**. He broke into the Norwich team just in time for their first European campaign.

But the end was very different. When 26 knee operations culminated in him retiring at 28, a period of bleak depression overwhelmed him.

Ultimately, though, he won that battle, just as he used to beat full backs – and this is his frank but inspiring tale.

MISSING BUSES AND MISSING THE GAME

BY DARREN EADIE

When I first lived in Norwich, I was 16. I signed forms as an apprentice, moved up to live in the city and shared digs with young Mr Jamie Cureton. That got a bit lively sometimes. I was a calming influence on Jamie, honestly! Somebody had to be.

He was the most naturally talented goalscorer I ever played with, and of course he's had a long career with lots of goals and lots of clubs, including two spells at Norwich. But perhaps it all came a bit too easily for him in some ways. He scored about 90 goals for two seasons in the Norwich youth team, but Jamie liked to go out. We all did, but Jamie really did.

We used to go by bus to training in the morning – or try to. We often missed it because Jamie wasn't ready in time. Our digs were near the Dolphin Bridge, off the Dereham Road. We'd nearly always have to run for the bus, but often we just missed it and so we just kept on running – all the way round to Trowse, which must have been more than three miles. We had to get a move on too, because we didn't dare be late for training. Perhaps all that extra running gave Jamie the stamina for his long career.

Our unintended extra stamina work amused a girl who was always on the same bus. She used to wave at us as it pulled away with us sprinting to try to get to the bus stop. She was on her way to her studies at City College, and Jamie and I must have managed to catch the bus a few times because I was able to ask this young lady out. We were both 17. We met at Ritzy's for our first date. I used to like a nice glass of Snakebite and Black. She was sick during the evening, but I still kissed her… classy!

We're still together. My poor, lovely wife Kelly didn't know what she was letting herself in for all those years ago.

Dave Stringer was the Norwich first team manager, Mike Walker was reserve team manager, and we had an incredible youth team squad. Andy Marshall was in goal, and there was Andy Johnson, Jamie, Ade Akinbiyi and me. All of us went on to play for the first team. There were at least a couple more who had pro careers elsewhere. Danny Mills was a couple of years behind us as well, and Craig Bellamy was a couple behind him. Chris Sutton was a year in front of me. That's a lot of seriously good players who came through the Norwich youth system – before the FA introduced restrictions on how far kids could travel to Centres of Excellence, so that clubs like Norwich had to stop the recruitment net being spread as widely.

I grew up in the West Country living in a pebble-dashed council house with my parents and my older brother. My mum and dad still live in Wiltshire, near to Bath. The Norwich chief executive at the time, Gordon Bennett, was a West Country man, and at Norwich he kept in touch with football down there and made sure there was a good scouting network. That's why Jamie, Craig Bellamy, Andy Johnson and some other decent West Country players found themselves at Carrow Road – or at least at Trowse, where the training ground was and where the youth teams played.

But I might have been a rugby player instead of a footballer. Where I grew up is rugby country, and I played scrum half for Bath Colts. I loved rugby. I was quick and could go around people.

In football, I was a Bristol Rovers fan, a 'Gashead'. I remember watching Rob Newman playing for our rivals, Bristol

City – they called themselves 'shitheads' and I'd agree! A few years later I was cleaning his boots when I was an apprentice at Norwich. He was a pretty decent tipper come Christmas time when we got a little bit of cash from the pros for looking after them.

I enjoyed all sports, but it was football I chose when I wanted to play outside the house with a ball, which was all of the time. My first inkling that perhaps I could play football professionally came when I was chosen for Swindon Town's Centre of Excellence at 11. I was still playing rugby at school, but I gave up Bath Colts. Mum says I made a conscious decision at 11 to choose football because there was more money in it!

A year later I switched to Southampton, which meant three-hour round trips for mum or dad to take me twice a week. As an under-13 at Saints, I played a match at Norwich. And a year later I signed for them, and two years later I moved to the city and started those unplanned morning runs to Trowse.

I progressed quickly. Dave Stringer was the first team manager, but he had managed the youth team and believed in giving youngsters a chance. He encouraged Mike Walker, who was in charge of the reserves, to pick us for his team. I got into Mike's team quite quickly and reserve team football then was brilliant. You played against seasoned pros. My first match was away to Chelsea. I was left midfield in a 4-4-2 and I was up against Steve Clarke at right back for Chelsea. He smashed me in the first minute, but I kind of knew that I had to man up. Thanks Steve.

Then, at the end of that season, which was 1991-92, Mike Walker took over as first team manager. It was an amazing period for Norwich. His first season was the start of the Premier League, and Norwich finished third.

For me, things got really going the following season, 1993-94. Obviously Mike knew all about the kids who had already stepped up into the reserves, because he'd been the reserves' manager, but, from a modern perspective, it does seems incredible that in his second season in charge he put me on the bench in the club's first ever European tie. I was only 18. It was the UEFA Cup first round home leg against Vitesse Arnhem in September 1993 – and I got on for the last 19 minutes. That was my senior debut: a European game!

That was just the start. We became the only English club team ever to win in Munich's Olympic Stadium when we beat Bayern. I was a sub for that game. And then I started up front for the second leg at our place. I remember standing in the tunnel before the start. We were on the left, and in the Bayern line, standing next to me on my right, is Lothar Matthäus. He'd won the World Cup as captain of Germany three years earlier.

Norwich completed another famous victory that night and, looking back at those two seasons – the one before I broke into the team and my first as a first teamer – were the most successful period of the Norwich City history. But I was 18, starting up front alongside Chris Sutton against Bayern, and I just thought it was going to be like that every week.

I scored on my Premier League debut, at QPR, and it was the stuff dreams were made of. Dave Phillips, who was the first choice for the left midfield position, was in negotiations with the club over a new contract and had thrown his toys out of the pram a bit. So Mike turned to me for the role, and knew I could play up top as well if necessary. Dave left, and the position was mine from then on, when I was fit.

It was a hell of a team. Ruel Fox was on the right. Chris Sutton and Efan Ekoku were usually up front, Ian Crook was in midfield, and behind me at left back was Mark Bowen. It was a great, attacking line-up. The way 'Chippy' Crook knew when 'Taffy' Bowen was going to make a run beyond me and into the box was like telepathy, it really was. And he could ping the ball into Taffy's stride at the precisely right moment.

We had a good mix of characters as well, with some older heads, like Gary Megson and Bryan Gunn. And of course Jeremy Goss scored some amazing goals. We never went onto a pitch with any fear. We always believed in each other.

Some of the players, the ones that had played a lot of seasons, had a sense that something special and probably unique for Norwich was going on but, as a teenager, I didn't think about it too much. I just went out and played and enjoyed myself. I have some absolutely brilliant memories of that team.

Because so many good youngsters were rolling off the production line, I believe the board at the time thought, 'Well we can sell so-and-so because there'll be another one along in a short while'. So the work of good football men, like Dave Stringer, Mike Walker and so-on kept the club in the top division and doing well.

But you can't go on selling your best players because, eventually, there isn't another one coming along. I think the rot set in when Robert Chase, the chairman, who had said he wouldn't sell Chris Sutton, decided to do so because the bid, £5 million from Blackburn, was too good to turn down. Mike Walker had already gone, Foxy went... and the season after beating Bayern, Norwich were relegated.

Things didn't go well in the second tier. Martin O'Neill was appointed manager and might well have turned things round but when we played at Leicester (I scored, by the way), Martin never turned up for the team meeting and we learned later he'd gone. Soon afterwards, he became Leicester manager.

If you count 'caretakers' I had 11 first team managers at Norwich in six years – but only nine different men, because both Gary Megson and Mike Walker had two spells in charge. That's still a crazy turnover, and it shows how difficult things had become at the club.

Robert Chase wasn't popular with the fans and the

demonstrations and ill feeling became so bad that, in the end, he resigned. But I have to be honest and say he was great for the players. When I was in the England under-21 squad, I was picked for the Toulon tournament in France. Robert Chase flew my mum and Kelly, my girlfriend as she was then, in his private jet and put them up in a hotel in St Tropez. We won the tournament by the way, just like the England under-21s did in 2016.

At the same time, I started getting my knee injuries. I picked up one when I was with the England senior squad. I was called up to go to the Tournoi tournament in France in the summer of 1997 by Glenn Hoddle – the one in which Roberto Carlos scored an amazing free kick for Brazil against France. I'd had probably my best year with Norwich and been voted player-of-the-season and was top scorer with 19 goals. When the England squad all got together, an official photograph was taken, and I was in it, alongside Paul Gascoigne, David Beckham, Paul Scholes, Alan Shearer, Ian Wright and players like that. But then I got injured during a training session and didn't go to France for the tournament. England won it, too.

I must have been a half decent player, mustn't I? And I suppose that made it harder to take when it all ended when I was still young because of my knee – although when the injuries and the operations started coming, I always thought I'd get back to playing, and that it would be Norwich that I would play for.

Then my final Norwich manager, Bruce Rioch, called me in and told me the club had accepted a bid from Leicester. I genuinely didn't want to go. He said I could go and talk to them but I said, 'One hundred per cent I am not going.' Bruce told me that if I didn't, the club would go into administration. The bid was a Leicester record of £3 million and Norwich had debts of about £7 million, apparently. I'd had about 15 operations on my knee by then, too.

It was December 1999. Norwich fans weren't happy that I went but I don't think they blamed me and from my point of view I didn't feel I had any choice. Delia Smith sent me a postcard saying she was sorry I was going, and drew a little picture of someone crying. She is such a fantastic lady and I have a huge amount of love for her.

In Leicester, we bought a house just off the A47 so that we could get back to Norwich easily when we wanted to. I'd have been happy finishing my career with Norwich, and I thought that perhaps I still could. I thought I could have a stay at Leicester and then come back for the end of my career.

Linking up with Martin O'Neill at Leicester would be good though, I thought.

On the day I signed, I had to have a scan on my knee because I'd already had so many operations. The specialist said, 'He could last six years. He could last six months. I can't say.' Martin O'Neill said, 'I don't care. I want to sign him.' That was a tremendous boost. My dad is Leicester born and bred and a massive Foxes fan, so he was delighted I was on the move to his boyhood club.

But I only played 40-odd matches in four years at Leicester. The operations kept coming, and I don't know whether there was some underlying weakness, or it was just a culmination of lots of knocks. I don't know what started the trouble, but I do know what started the beginning of the end. Scott Parker, playing for Charlton against Leicester, absolutely smashed me. I went off on a stretcher and I never really came back from that, although I didn't know that when it happened. Scott came and apologised and I've put the issue of his involvement in my troubles to bed. It doesn't do any good to think about it.

So the way football ended for me wasn't great. I had a total of 26 operations on my left knee. One period of rehab lasted a full year, and any player will tell you that dealing with long-term injury is the hardest thing to do. You're still part of the squad but you're not really. You don't train with the others, you don't go to away games and above all, you don't play; you're not a proper part of the match day. You're not in the changing room with them. You're definitely not out on the pitch with them. There's still a rhythm to the week, but it feels like a longer week, and while the lads are recovering from a game and building up to the next one, you're doing the same stuff every day. I would go to the training ground and see the other lads go out training. They'd come in at ten and probably be finished by 12. But I was getting in at half-nine and I'd be doing my rehab until five.

In the early part of that year's rehab, I was on a machine bending my knee for literally eight hours a day. I had no control over it. I was just lying there and this machine was bending my leg. My knee didn't want to be bent but the machine was bending it, and I was in a lot of pain. It was mindnumbingly boring as well and, frankly, it gave me too much time to think, to retreat into my own mind and go through all the 'what ifs'. Eight hours a day thinking and having my knee bent back and forth. It went on and on. My son, Taylor, had his sixth birthday while I was spending my days like that. He saw me doing that on the machine, and he knew what was going on. He was upset about it. I know it affected others around me just as much too.

I kept going because I thought I could get fit enough to play. I'd always come back from operations, so I thought I could keep doing that. Eventually, though, I lost the confidence that I would ever play again. But I kept going until it was obvious that there was no point. If you break open a joint of meat and see the shiny bits on the end of the bone, that is what the final lot of operations tried to sort out: the articular cartilage. There were three areas that needed repair, and the most innovative way that offered hope was to take slivers of bone from my shin, each of them probably the size of a five pence piece.

They injected each sliver with tissue that had been taken from my knee in previous operations and grafted the three slivers onto the problem areas of the knee. The world leader in this operation was Lars Peterson in Sweden. I went over to him to have it done. Then, after a while, I had another operation so that he could look at how the grafts had taken. He said they had hardened up nicely and that he'd felt them and thought it was all fine.

I started training, but during a run I felt something go. I was lying there on the training field and I could see this lump on my knee and could push it around under the skin. It was one of the slivers of bone that had been grafted on. It hadn't knitted in properly. And I realised that the other two would go as well. Eventually they did.

When you finish playing, they call it 'hanging your boots up'. But I didn't hang mine up. On the last day I left the training ground, I took my boots off the peg and took them home with me, and my shin-pads. I don't know why.

I'd made that journey from the training ground to my home so many times, and so everything was familiar as I left that last time, but for me it felt very different this time. I've only been back to that training ground in Leicester once in the 11 years since. We moved back to Norwich soon after. Kelly is a Norwich girl after all, and we'd always wanted and intended to move back eventually, so that is what we did. There was no point in staying near Leicester any more.

Back in Norwich, I didn't really get involved in the football at all. I didn't even watch it on the telly. If I did accept an invitation to go to a Carrow Road game, if I am honest, I hated it, because I wanted to go out and play. I hated all the passion, because I was no longer part of it. I was only 28. People would joke, 'Get your boots on Eadie', and stuff like that. They'd say, 'We wish you were out there'. They meant it as a compliment.

But the person who really wished I was out there was me.

A football ground on match day has a special feel. There's the noise, the smell, the excitement and tension in the air. In the dressing room area there is the smell of liniment. Ever since I could remember, football was all I'd done, and going to the ground on match day really drummed it home to me that I was no longer part of it. So, sorry, but no, I didn't want to watch my mates playing. It became torture. My plan had always been to finish my career with a two or three-season swansong at Norwich. But now my career WAS finished, I didn't want to be there at all. I thought I should step away from football completely, but that idea just made the same question go round and round in my head: 'So what am I going to do?'.

As a footballer you are taught to have that little bit of anxiety, a little bit of an edge, because it got you up for a game. So I didn't really think, once I'd stopped, that all the anxiety I was feeling was wrong. But it took over.

There was an accumulation of things. I had the extreme disappointment of not being able to play any more and then I was involved in a business that didn't do very well because of somebody else. I lost money, but I also lost my trust in people, and that was a big thing because trust is massive in football. I'd gone from school to a football environment in which you had to trust your team-mates. You trusted everyone at the club to be on your side. You trusted people to do things for you. It was all about trust, and when I left that environment, I assumed I could go on trusting people around me but found out pretty quickly there were a lot of people you can't.

Another thing was that in football you have decisions made for you and things done for you. The club want you to be able to just concentrate on the game. So when I finished playing I sat down and said to Kelly, 'Look, I have no idea how to sort out a passport. If we go on holiday, I have no idea how you go about arranging that. I have never done anything like that'. I didn't know anything about getting a car, or organising anything that needed doing to the house. I had no idea about any of the ordinary things people have to do.

I suppose that will seem arrogant. I'd had everything done for me, and everyone outside the game has to get on and do things for themselves. But I'd had no say in it. All the day-to-day stuff is taken on by those around you so that you are concentrating on nothing but your football. That was just the way it was. And then, suddenly, that wasn't the way it was.

I understand the perception of ex-footballers is that they all go out gambling, taking drugs, having drink problems, but for a lot of them that behaviour is escapism. They can't play any more and don't get the incredible high of playing the game. And it's more than just not being able to play football any more. They've lost their purpose of life. That's what it was like for me, certainly.

I kept telling myself and others that I was fine, but my worries and fears accumulated.

Then came the news that my mum had been diagnosed with breast cancer and I just couldn't cope any more. Thoughts were going round in my head all the time. Too many things. I couldn't sleep. As soon as I stopped thinking about something, I'd start thinking about it again. My brain had trained itself to be like that. And the more it behaved like that, the more the chemicals in the brain got out of balance. So the more the destructive thought processes continued.

If you feed your body crap, you get fat. I was feeding my mind with bad thoughts and continuous anxiety and it trained itself to be that way. It became 'normal' for me to have the same scenarios playing out in my mind all the time. And when you can't sleep, the sleep deprivation is terribly debilitating as well. 'Nothingness' is probably the correct word to describe how I felt. I got to the point where my panic attacks were stopping me living properly. When you are like that you can't get yourself up. You can't shave. You just can't do it. You want to shut yourself away. I was ringing Kelly and asking her to pick me up from the city because I couldn't drive myself home. I couldn't go into the garden to play with our son, Taylor. I couldn't go into the sea when we were on a family holiday. I just couldn't. I was getting cold feelings on the top of my head and pins and needles in my hands: physical signs of how ill my mind had become, I suppose.

It was very hard for my wife. I became like another child to her. We have three kids but I was probably the hardest work. Nothing had prepared her for this. She wasn't a trained nurse or anything. But she had to cope to keep the family going.

Eventually she persuaded me to find some help. But I didn't want to speak to a psychiatrist. I didn't want to speak to some-one who I thought was going to judge me.

I remembered that Leon McKenzie had spoken about his mental struggles. I never played with him at Norwich, but I knew him through our mutual Carrow Road connection. So I rang him and we talked for a long time. Of course he under-stood exactly what I was going through, not only because he'd had a similar illness, but because he'd been a footballer and so the causes were similar too.

Leon put me on to Clarke Carlisle, who was PFA chairman at the time and had suffered his own demons. He said he would get someone to ring me. So I was with my wife in the fruit aisle in Marks and Spencer in Norwich when my phone rang. I didn't recognise the number so I thought, 'This must be it. I am finally going to get some help, after all this time'.

It was Peter Kay, who had founded the Sporting Chance clinic with ex-footballer Tony Adams. But actually the clinic is specifically for people with addictions – drink, drugs, gambling.

We talked for a while but he explained pretty much straight away that his clinic couldn't help me. He told me the best thing I could do would be to go and see my doctor.

That was another hammer blow. I'd thought the call would be the start of getting better, but it wasn't at all. And it was around that time that Wales manager Gary Speed took his own life. He was just 42. I had never got to that point. I didn't think I could put my wife and family through that. I had told my wife I wasn't thinking like that. But if the PFA couldn't help me, well… I started to doubt myself. I thought, 'I don't imagine Gary Speed thought he'd ever feel he had to take his own life, so how can I be sure that I won't ever feel like that?'

Finally, with nowhere else to turn, I managed to go to see my own local doctor. And he was absolutely amazing. He still is, in fact. I still see him regularly when I need to. He put me in touch with the right people and got me on the medication that was right for me. The medication was absolutely key. People are afraid of taking tablets that 'affect your mind' because they think that is a weakness, or will lead to addiction or something. But people don't worry about taking tablets for migraine. And the right medication can definitely help with anxiety and depression. Mine don't change who I am. They just take the edge off and stop me getting too low or too high. You certainly do have to get the ones that are right for you. I was prescribed some that sent me the other way – made me worse – but once I got the right medication, I started to feel released from a nightmare. I was able to start to retrain my mind and get back into a better sleep pattern.

It is a long road. I still have times when things happen and I get anxious again. It's never anywhere near as bad as it was before I went to see my doctor, but it is a problem I live with rather than one that goes away completely for good. But I assure you if you are having problems, it does get better even though it feels like it never will. I would say to anyone who starts to feel unwell in this way is that there is absolutely nothing to be ashamed about. I'd particularly make that point to footballers. Depression and anxiety – and I'm using the clinical terms, not talking about feeling a little bit low or a bit worried – are very, very common. It's in all walks of life, and I wouldn't want people to think I'm saying sports people get it worse, but I do think a particular issue for professional sportspeople is that the end of your career can be a real jolt.

You are drilled, throughout your life, into thinking you will be a footballer. That's what you are told as a kid when you are doing well. So football is all that matters.

Then the ones that are successful get to fulfil their dreams and have an enviable lifestyle and everything, but many, many others don't. So at that point when you finish, whether it's through not making the grade, injury or you just reach the end of your career, that's the point in your life when the thing you've done, the person you've been, just stops. I needed to find a new 'Darren Eadie.' The footballer one was gone for me at 28.

And because football is a blokey, macho environment, some players find it very difficult to say, 'I'm unwell and need help'. But unless you do say that, things will get worse. It's hard to tell people you're struggling, because people don't talk about mental health issues. There's a stigma about depression, and about clinics. It's bizarre, but I was the same when I started feeling like it. I kept it to myself and didn't want to talk to anyone about it. I'd put on my okay face and go out and nobody would know. But talking about it is important, because people who suddenly start to suffer need to know that it is really very, very common. And there is help out there for them. So, if I could make just one person in a hundred million to feel a little easier about it, then that would be great.

With the help of my doctor, and with Kelly's amazing

support, things got better. I got my love of football back. Watching Leicester's incredible Premier League season in 2015-16 helped. And I really enjoy my involvement with my first club, Norwich, through working for Mustard TV and many other media outlets like Sky, talkSPORT, BT sport and Radio Norfolk.

I am also head of football at Langley School, an independent school in Loddon where I run a football academy. The school is an education partner with Norwich City and 24 NCFC academy lads attend the school and play for the school team. I hope to share my experiences, good and bad with them. After all I have been there and done it, through the whole system from bottom to top. That is vital to their development in my opinion.

So, if I could go back in time and be that 11-year-old boy in that house near Bath, and I had to decide between football, rugby or some other path, what would I choose? If I knew all that I know now, that the football would end so prematurely with all the injuries, and that the end would pitch me into depression, what would I choose? I would still choose football. I don't have any doubt in my mind. Anybody who has the opportunity to go and do it should do it. It's the best life in the world. I'd do it all again because it was amazing, despite the hard times, and it gave me the family I have today – and that is the most important outcome.

Darren Eadie scored 38 goals in 204 Norwich appearances between 1992 and 1999. He was too good for the then cash-strapped club to keep, but, after a big-money move to Leicester, he had to retire at 28 through injury. He now works at Langley School, Loddon, and makes regular appearances on Mustard TV and other media outlets.

10

Craig Fleming spent ten years at Norwich and made almost 400 appearances.

Despite needing to be patched up regularly, he did not miss a single league game for two entire seasons – and it is one of those seasons that he focuses on in his tale: City's surge to the Football League title in 2003-04.

What did manager Nigel Worthington say that made such a difference towards the end of the campaign?

THE PERFECT STORM

BY CRAIG FLEMING

When I left Norwich in 2007 I gave an interview and said winning promotion in 2004 had been the highlight. Now, looking back, I am even more certain of that. In fact, it was the highlight of my entire playing career, not just my decade at Norwich. It was special because of how everything came together: so many ingredients all being there at the right time. I describe it as being like a perfect storm, when a set of lots of circumstances happened and created something that was unique.

I had quite a lot of success before I played for Norwich. In fact I had a success right at the start. I made my debut for Halifax, my home-town club, at 16 – as substitute in the tournament that became the Johnstone's Paint Trophy. The game went to penalties and I scored the winning spot kick!

I had been at Nottingham Forest as a schoolboy, in the Brian Clough era, but my brother Paul, who is four years older than me, was at Halifax and they offered me a YTS contract when I was 14. I made my full league debut in the same season as that penalty success, while I was still just 16.

I also had success at Oldham under Joe Royle. We had three seasons in the Premier League and I played at Wembley in an FA Cup semi-final. The semi was in 1994, against Manchester United. We were winning but Mark Hughes scored in the very last minute of extra-time and we got thumped in the replay. But I was 22 and it was brilliant to be a part of the good things that happened at Oldham in the six years I was there.

I had been diagnosed with a double hernia during that cup semi-final season but carried on playing and then, because everything else was compensating for that injury, I developed major complications affecting my groin and hip. I had been flying, but I was out for nine months.

I got myself fit and playing again, but things were not going well for Oldham and it was Joe Royle who more or less persuaded me to go to Norwich, after the 1996-97 season. Oldham were in the second tier and the last game of the season, at Boundary Park, was against Norwich. Oldham were already relegated by then, and Norwich won 3-0, but I must have had a good game, because that summer, I heard that Mickey Walker, who was in his second spell as Norwich manager, was talking about me. Mike Phelan and Neil Adams were both at Carrow Road and I knew them both. They rang me and said the manger had been asking questions about me, so I knew I was on the Norwich radar. Joe Royle had left Oldham and, in fact, had just lost his job at Everton. I talked to him about Norwich and he said, 'If you get the chance to go, you'll love it and end up staying'. So I did go, and I did stay: for ten years.

When I arrived, Norwich had the remnants of the side who had played in Europe. There were players like Darren Eadie in the team and there were also some decent youngsters coming though, including Craig Bellamy. My partner in the centre of defence was Matt Jackson, and he was a hell of a player. But we only finished 15th and Mickey Walker lost his job just before the end of the season.

Bruce Rioch took over before the next season, 1998-99. He was someone you wouldn't want to get on the wrong side of – very strict – but I had a lot of time for him and thought we might be able to get somewhere with him.

We were stuck in mid-table in the second tier, though, and

when Bryan Hamilton took over it wasn't a great time to be
at the club. The dressing room became fragmented and, to be
honest, some of the players who arrived during that era weren't
great. We became a poor team.

When Nigel Worthington stepped up from Bryan's assistant
to the top job, in December 2000, things started to feel very
different. The best thing Nigel did was he saw the problems
and dealt with them quickly. Players he didn't think were good
enough were moved out sharply. Players who weren't great in
the dressing room went too.

Nigel changed the training; he made it sharper with more
tempo. They were tough sessions and we became fitter. My
philosophy is that football is a massively aerobic sport and
you need to be fit to do it. So with Nigel in charge and Dave
Carolan working as the fitness coach, it suited me and the team
definitely became fitter.

Nigel kept us up that season. Then, in his first full season,
we reached the play-off final for promotion to the Premier
League. And that was the season, 2001-02, that my partnership
with Malky Mackay became established.

As a youngster I played in midfield. Early in my career I had
quite a lot of games at full back. But by the time Malky and I
paired up, I was a centre back. How it normally worked out
was that I would play alongside a big lump who wanted to go
and head everything and I would sweep around alongside him.
Malky was just one of many big lumps I played with.

No, he was a terrific player. We used to argue like cat and
dog and blame each other for every goal that went in, and there
was a rivalry too. But we were kind of built for each other. The
deficiencies that Malky had were my strengths, and my deficiencies were Malky's strengths. We just complemented each other.

I like to think I have a good football brain. I needed one,
because the bad injury I'd had at Oldham had slowed me down.

Before the injury, I didn't necessarily understand the game fully, but I had electric pace and could make up for getting things wrong with my athleticism. Post injury I had to play differently. I lost half a yard, and if I was out of position I couldn't recover from it, so I learned to read the game and get my positioning right.

I was not the tallest centre half, and after my injury, not the very quickest, so I had to use my brain. I would think about the striker I was going to play against and consider how I would combat him. For instance, with some players I would try and nick the ball before he could try and roll me.

Malky has a good football brain too and we would talk about certain situations and discuss how to deal with them. There was definitely a competitive element between us too. We both wanted to be the best defender in the side, and that was a good thing. We didn't socialise together all the time, or anything like that, but if the lads had a night out me and him would certainly be together at the bar – although with him being a Scot and me being from Yorkshire it wasn't exactly a race to buy a round.

In that 2001-02 season we played Wolves in the play-off semi-finals. Malky scored in the last minute of the first leg, at Carrow Road, to make it 3-1. That meant they would have to score twice against us at Molineux to stop us going through and in our defence there was a real belief that we could stop that happening. Malky and I knew each other's game really well, Darren Kenton was playing well at right back, Adam Drury was an exceptional left back and Rob Green was a great goalkeeper.

There's a saying about 'the ground rocked' and it really did feel as if it was shaking that night when Kevin Cooper scored for them with about a quarter of an hour left. But we kept them out for the rest of the match and went through to the final, at the Millennium Stadium, Cardiff.

But we lost to Birmingham on penalties and some of us

thought, 'That's our chance of playing in the Premier League gone'. Iwan Roberts and me are both fairly solid guys but we were both crying like babies.

The following season there was a kind of a backlash after losing at the Millennium. We finished just outside the play-off positions and me and Malky got quite a lot of stick from fans. Norwich is a small place, and I'd been there a long time. If supporters were against me, I knew. There was no escape from it. And after we'd lost in the play-off final, fans thought some of us were too old. But I knew my legs hadn't gone and I had some time left, so it made me more determined. I am glad I stuck around, because the next season, 2003-04, brought that perfect storm – and it blew us to the title.

One of the ingredients was 'Steady Eddie': Marc Edworthy, who came in at right back and was my room-mate. He was like Denis Irwin was for Manchester United, dependable and consistent. He defended well, he was good in possession, and he got up and down the wing.

The rest of the defence was still 'Greeno' in goal, me, Malky and Adam. Nigel made Adam captain and I think that was a masterstroke. We already had leaders everywhere on the pitch – me, Malky, Iwan, Gary Holt, Phil Mulryne – and Adam was already the best left back outside the Premier League. But making him captain added something to his game. It was another part of the perfect storm.

One more element was that we didn't get injuries, particularly in defence. Or, if we did, we just kept going. I had a dodgy hip and knee, and a back which kept seizing up. I lost count of how many times I had stitches during a game for a head wound. But I didn't miss a league game for two seasons: that 2003-04 campaign or the following season in the Premier League. I was probably one of the first footballers to take up yoga, and I used to swim after training. I used to look after myself. I still flew into tackles when I had to, but you just grind through the injuries. Malky was the same. And so were Eddie, Adam and Holt. We just weren't a team who would give in to injuries.

Another component was the positivity throughout the club. We did lose games that season. We lost at Northampton in the League Cup and experienced that 'This is not good enough' feeling among the fans. But mostly defeats didn't cause negativity. Everyone – fans, players, the board, people who worked at the club – all seemed positive. As a player, you are definitely aware if the fans are with you. And, mostly, if we went 1-0 down that season there were no moans and groans in the crowd. We all thought, 'We can still win this', and the crowd was part of that, definitely.

There was a game at Burnley in the April. It was 3-2 to them at half-time. The dressing rooms were under the away end, where our fans kept singing and chanting all the way through half-time. We ended up winning 5-3.

Looking back, losing at the Millennium in the 2002 play-off final was the beginning of a new level of support for Norwich City. People talk about the full houses at Carrow Road, but when I first went there we were getting crowds of 14,000 or 15,000. People like Andy Cullen, who was director of sales and marketing, worked hard to capitalise on the potential fan-base and reaching the play-off final ignited the support. Then the new Jarrold Stand was opened during the 2003-04 season, increasing Carrow Road's capacity. That helped the perfect storm too.

Another big factor was that we all blended in the dressing room as well as on the pitch. There were no cliques or little groups. We were really together and we fancied our chances that season.

There is no doubt that getting Peter Crouch and Darren Huckerby on loan in September was another massive factor.

Crouchy was certainly massively tall. For his first game (a win at Gillingham) the club had to have extensions sewn onto the bottom of his shorts until they could get a few pairs especially manufactured.

We already felt we had the basis of a team that should be able to challenge for promotion. We were solid, consistent and hard to beat. But we didn't have that little bit of magic that could turn a tight game into a win – until Crouchy and Hucks came. Then we were transformed. We were electric. All of a sudden, if we were defending and got hold of the ball on the edge of our box, we could pick out Iwan or Crouch. Or Hucks would take the ball from the edge of our box to the edge of theirs. We became a dangerous side to play against.

Hucks scored an amazing goal against Cardiff. I scored as well, but for some reason people remember Hucks taking the ball from the halfway line to score his goal!

That was supposed to be his last game, because his loan from Manchester City was over. Crouchy was going back to Aston Villa too. I was devastated. We all were, because we could see what would be possible if either or both of them stayed. I spoke to Nigel and he was really anxious that we might lose that momentum and belief. But, fair play to the club, they put a deal together to get Hucks back. Apparently Kevin Keegan, the Manchester City manager was really helpful, and that was yet another thing adding to our perfect storm.

With Hucks, his defending was practically non-existent, so you didn't want him anywhere near our goal because he was a liability. But he gave us something special in attack – where Iwan was already the best target man I had played with.

If I was on the ball but getting closed down by a centre forward, then two central midfielders would drop back towards me to take the ball. If their markers didn't track them, I would give the ball to one of our midfielders. But their markers usually did track them towards our area, and that left space behind them. So I would dink the ball over their heads, onto Iwan's chest. You knew it would stick and the lads would play off him.

In midfield we had Holty, Damien Francis and Phil Mulryne: all very different but they complemented each other really well and it was a goal by Phil that made me believe we would go up.

It was at Reading in the April. A couple of days beforehand my back had gone completely. I couldn't straighten up at all. I had a back specialist I used to see, and he treated me, but I travelled to that game with Neal Reynolds, the Norwich physio. I played, and it was a really tight game. There was no score for 85 minutes but then the referee, Neale Barry, got in the way of a defensive header and the ball bounced off the ref to Mullers, just inside the area. He hit it on the half-volley, won the game, and put us on top of the table. After an 'assist' by a ref, I thought, 'This is definitely our year!'

But really, we'd believed in ourselves all season, and belief is huge in football because the game is about very small margins: fractions. So if you are not feeling confident, and you stand a couple of yards off your man, you never seem to be able to make that interception. It's not about lack of effort: it is about feeling confident enough to mark tighter. It's the same with passes; a confident player will hit them crisply, but someone lacking belief will pass more tentatively.

Another factor is pressure. If you are frightened of losing, then you become frightened to play, and so, if there are two passing options, you take the easier one – because you don't want to risk a mistake. In that 2003-04 season, we had confidence but not fear. We went onto the pitch thinking, 'We'll get something here'.

We weren't over confident, though. Whilst there was, deep

down, the feeling that we would do it, we never stopped looking over our shoulders.

Sometimes you will hear managers say they have banned their team from talking about winning promotion, or winning the cup, or the title – whatever it is they are in with a chance of. But we certainly talked about winning promotion and the title that season. We were encouraged to do so.

We did some work with Keith Mincher, a sports psychologist who was with the England under-21s. I worked very closely with him and thought he was excellent. He told me, and some of the other experienced players, to drop little comments about winning into conversations. So we'd say things like, 'It will be amazing if we win the league'.

Another of Keith's little gambits was to get us to keep playing the same music after games. Jimmy Brennan was in charge of the music and played Sweet Home Alabama a couple of time after wins. Keith told him to keep playing it, so that it reinforced the feeling that we were winning a lot – which we were.

As we got closer to promotion, the club started flying us to away games. Nigel asked for it and the board said yes. As supporters know, everywhere is so far from Norwich by road. I remember one away game when I was at Norwich, at Burnley, being cancelled and yet we still didn't get back to Norwich until very nearly six in the morning. That sort of thing takes it out of you. So flying made a real difference. All these little things added to the big things and whipped up that perfect storm.

That 5-3 win at Burnley was at the start of April, and turned out to be the second of seven wins on the spin. So we clinched promotion, with weeks to spare. And, once we knew we were going up into the Premier League, we were ready to say, 'That's it. Season finished'. It had been a long slog, and we were a really tight-knit group of players and, to be honest, we drank Norwich dry for about two days solid.

We could quite easily have just taken the promotion and not bothered with the title. But Nigel said to us, 'Not many footballers finish their careers having won a title. You might only get one chance in life to win a medal. We have this chance now. So we are not going to take our foot off the gas. We are going to train even harder. We are going to win the league.' I will always be in Nigel's debt because he said that. Without it, I wouldn't have my winner's medal. His attitude and that pep talk were the final two elements of the perfect storm.

The title was still up for grabs when we reached the penultimate game: a Tuesday night match at Sunderland, who had just missed out on automatic promotion.

They got a goal after 44 minutes and all hell broke out in our dressing room at half-time. Nigel was screaming, 'That's not good enough!' Hucks kicked off with Nigel. Iwan and Leon McKenzie had an argument about something. Nigel kicked the metal skip, thinking it would be empty and light, but it was full of kit and we all thought he had broken his foot. It was absolute bedlam.

But that shows what we were like, how determined we were and what Nigel had created. Then, in the second half the cheers from our fans at the away end told us something was going on and when we came off at the end, we learned that West Brom, our only rivals for the title, had lost heavily at Stoke. We were champions.

I'd had some great times as a footballer, particularly the cup runs at Oldham, and we'd also had a great escape at Oldham, winning the last three games to stay up, but that night at Sunderland was the best feeling I had as a player.

It doesn't matter what league you are in, winning it is incredible. It's a season's work. So winning the Football League was absolutely the best footballing thing I did. It was just amazing. The club had waited so long for it and a few of us players had been through the mill a bit. But we were the champions.

There was one game left though: away to Crewe. I scored and did a belly-flop dive in front of our fans but again someone else nicked the headlines. It was Iwan's last game and he scored goals 95 and 96 for Norwich. The first was an absolute beauty. The second was a twice-taken penalty.

We had been drinking – of course we had; we'd flown back from Sunderland the previous Tuesday and gone straight out and partied – but we played the best football we had played all season at Crewe. They were a footballing team but we passed them to death. It was a special, surreal feeling: no pressure at all, exhilarated by what we'd already achieved, just playing total football.

The final table showed us on 94 points from 46 games with a positive goal difference of 40. Second-placed West Brom had eight points fewer. Sunderland finished third with 79 points. We had blitzed it.

The supporters voted me player of the season and that meant a lot to me. I had been second and third before, but winning it was very special. I was at my post-injury peak as a player and for the fans to think I'd contributed enough to be their man of the season was truly memorable.

But in the summer, to be honest, the exceptional feelings we all had as a group of players began to dissipate. Malky and Iwan left the club, which meant our tight-knit group was breaking up. I went for a farewell drink with Malky and it seemed like the perfect storm had blown itself out.

Of course I relished the challenge of playing in the Premier League and, once we'd signed Dean Ashton at the turn of the year, it looked as if we might stay up. But we didn't and, of course, that tarnished the achievement of the previous season to a certain extent. Winning that title remains something I look back on with pride though, and with some great memories.

I stayed at Norwich until January 2007. I'd played 382 games, been captain, club captain and player of the season, and I am a member of the club's Hall of Fame. I am proud of all that and Norwich City was a huge part of my life.

I tried to give something back, too. When I was captain I accepted several opportunities to do things for and with charities and after I left I did a 203-mile 'Hike and Bike' for two local charities. Lots of footballers support charities, and I was really pleased to be able to help.

I left initially to join Wolves on loan, but then was recalled by Norwich and released so that I could sign for Rotherham, for whom I played 17 times. Next I returned to Norfolk to play for King's Lynn, but that didn't really work out. My heart wasn't in it and my body wasn't right. I decided to pack it in.

I had fallen out of love with football a little bit. Some of the old-school values that I revered had changed, I felt.

But I had always had a mind to take up coaching. I had done my badges while I was at Oldham, and in fact did some coaching at that stage at the Manchester United academy, under Eric Harrison, the man behind the famous class of 1992, which included the Neville brothers, David Beckham, Nicky Butt and Paul Scholes.

So, just before the 2008-09 season, a call from Lowestoft Town helped rekindle my affection for the game. They wanted me to play for them, but when I said that wasn't really an option because of an ankle injury, they offered me a coaching position.

The players were all local lads, working during the day and coming to train in the evenings. We won two promotions, and I had been promoted to director of football by the time we got a third promotion, to the Conference North.

Then Martin Hunter got in touch. He was caretaker manager at Norwich when Nigel left, but I already knew him from when I was at Oldham and he was one of the FA's regional directors of coaching. We got on well and he said that if he was ever in a position to offer me a coaching job, he would do so. And that is what he did when he began working at Southampton.

He is technical director, working closely with Les Reed, who is head of the very successful Saints academy. I am in charge of the under-18s and it is certainly a full-on job. I have learned so much; it is like going to school every day. It is a very different life from being a player, and means I now have different priorities, because the main focus is not winning games, it is developing players.

But, although it's tucked away somewhere at home and I don't look at it very often, I have got a medal for winning. Thank you Nigel.

Craig Fleming made almost 600 league appearances for a total of five clubs, but 343 of them were during ten years as a Norwich player. He was captain, club captain, and player of the season and was elected to City's Hall Of Fame. After retiring as a player he was a successful coach at Lowestoft Town and is currently working at Southampton's well-regarded academy.

Who says politics and sport shouldn't mix? **Ed Balls** used to make sure they did. When he and Chancellor of the Exchequer Gordon Brown were on important trips to the US they would make sure they found a bar showing English games.

This is the tale of how a man who used to sit in the Cabinet remembers standing on the terraces, how generations of his family have supported Norwich City and how he came to be offered the job of chairing the club he cares about.

MY FAMILY, OUR CLUB, MY HONOUR

BY ED BALLS

Easter Saturday 1976 was one of my greatest ever Norwich City footballing days. And not simply because we were at Carrow Road to see Norwich beat QPR 3-2 and deny them the top division title, with my hero, Ted MacDougall, scoring the opening goal.

The reason, it was extra special came ten minutes after we returned home to my uncle Frank's house in Sheringham. My aunt was laying out the tea when the doorbell rang and a man handed me a Norwich City yellow and green panelled football. 'Congratulations,' he said. 'Your uncle bought you a ticket for the RNLI lifeboat raffle and here is the winning prize, a match ball signed by all the Norwich City players'.

What a win! When we returned back to our home in Nottingham, my new ball had pride of place on my bedroom shelf. And there it sat – beautiful, precious and so tantalising. Every day when I looked at that ball, I wanted to take it outside and kick it. I was nine years old, playing football was my main pastime – and footballs weren't to be looked at or treasured.

It took three weeks until I cracked. One Sunday afternoon, when mum and dad were out, a few friends called round and I told them I had a new ball, 'a proper leather one with panels and everything'. We went up to our village recreation ground and I alternately imagined myself as Ted MacDougall, Graham Paddon, Colin Suggett, Duncan Forbes, even Kevin Keelan doing his famous double scissor-kick. When we finally walked home, my ball was nicely scuffed, all the signatures had been rubbed off, it was no longer a possession to be kept on the shelf, but it had been used for its true purpose – playing football.

I found out 20 years later, shortly after his death, that my uncle Frank hadn't actually bought a raffle ticket at all. He'd been to a fundraising dinner the week before, bid in the auction for the signed football and then arranged for a neighbour to come round after the QPR game with a raffle ticket and the ball. That was my brilliant, thoughtful, Norwich City-obsessed uncle all over.

I never actually went to a Norwich City home game with uncle Frank. He had a season ticket for more than 50 years just below the directors' box in the City stand. I had to rely upon other family members for my football tickets. My mum and dad were born and bred in Norwich – my mum growing up above a butcher's shop on Unthank Road and going to Notre Dame girls' school; my dad in a terraced house off Newmarket Road, and winning a scholarship to the City of Norwich School. Both their families were full of Norwich City fans, so much so that when the day I was due to be born – February 18, 1967 – clashed with a fourth round FA cup tie at Manchester United, the family decided that my dad was better off going to the game. I am sure my long-suffering mother would have just rolled her eyes. Luckily I arrived a week late.

It was my mum's brother-in-law, uncle John Gunton, who arranged for my first game at Carrow Road, in January 1973. First, though, I was to be given a trial run to see whether this six year old could sit still for the full 90 minutes. The Saturday before the game, we drove over to their house in March, Cambridgeshire, and I was sent off with my dad, uncle John and my cousin Robert to watch March versus Wisbech Town. I had a scarf, hat, a huge rattle, a comic and a large bag of pear drops. I think they thought I was going to be bored to death.

We probably doubled the usual home attendance. And while I can't remember anything about the game at all, I do know that I watched avidly – and passed the test.

The next weekend we went to see Don Revie's mighty Leeds at Carrow Road in the FA Cup third round in front of 32,310. Norwich drew 1-1, but again I don't remember much about the actual game. What I do remember vividly is walking to the ground in a growing mass of supporters, who all seemed twice as tall as me. I remember the surge of the crowd and the police hauling rowdy fans out of the stands. I remember the noise, the passion, the smell, how the singing bounced round the ground. It was the beginning of a lifetime of watching Norwich, and my initiation into our family love affair with the club.

We moved out of Norfolk in 1975, when my dad moved jobs from the University of East Anglia to the University of Nottingham, and I discovered how unusual it was to be a Norwich City supporter. Everyone in my old Bawburgh primary school class had been a Norwich City fan. Now I was the only one. And it turned out my sister, Joanna, and I also had a funny accent, with our East Midlands friends continually calling out 'Oo-Aah' whenever we spoke.

At first break, we went out to play football and I was tearing down the right wing in full Graham Paddon style when I put my foot just over the edge of the playground, slipped on what turned out to be very damp and muddy grass, and went flying. I was escorted back inside by one of the older girls, newspaper was laid out around the chair, and there I sat coated in thick mud for an hour until my mum arrived with a full change of clothes. Later that week I decided that I would turn up for the school assembly 'show and tell' in my full Norwich City kit. I stood decked out in yellow and green in front of 300 bemused children explaining where Norwich was and why I supported the Canaries.

After we moved, we regularly made the winding journey back to Norwich – through the Fens, via Thorney, Swaffham and Downham Market – for weddings, christenings, summer get-togethers. I don't know whether it was by accident or design but invariably these family 'dos' usually clashed with Norwich City matches and we always spent more time in the car park listening to Radio Norfolk than standing round the buffet.

I more often saw City play away in the late '70s and early '80s, against both Nottingham Forest and Notts County as well as at Filbert Street against Leicester, and a couple of times at Derby's Baseball Ground. One of my extra special memories is of a very tense, but exciting, exit from that stadium after a pulsating 2-2 draw in April 1977. Derby had been 2-0 up, and afterwards the frustrated Derby fans careered through the tight, terraced streets, with big police horses trying to keep order. We tried to stay safe standing on a front door step, rather regretting wearing our Norwich scarves.

We got back to my uncle John Gunton's car, and as he pulled out into the street a police officer noticed that I had my Norwich scarf trailing out of the window and beckoned us forward. Somehow, our little Morris Minor car ended up in the middle of the 10-coach-strong away supporters convoy. We were whisked out the city with a police escort, the fastest departure from Derby I've ever known. And as we pulled off the A52 at the Nottingham exit with our Norwich scarves streaming, we heard the honking of the coaches' horns waving us off in celebration of City's valuable point.

It's hard to imagine it now, but by the time I got to my mid-teens I had almost never seen Norwich City play live on TV. Back then, only the cup finals and England games were shown live. We got our football on the box from *Match of the Day* and *The Big Match*.

One rare live TV game was the 1975 League Cup final at

Wembley against Aston Villa, when Kevin Keelan pushed Ray
Graydon's penalty onto the post only to see him score from
the rebound. Villa one, Norwich nil. Ten years later, we had
the chance to make amends at Wembley against Sunderland in,
what by then was called the Milk Cup final. That time I was disappointed to have to watch the game on TV with my younger
brother, Andrew, as my dad only managed to get one ticket. It
was a great victory and, by the time my dad finally got home,
with a match programme for each of us, we were exhausted
from re-enacting the match in the back garden.

I had no choice but to be a Norwich City fan and nor
did Andrew. Seven years younger than me, he'd been only 18
months old when we moved to Nottingham, but he was a Norwich City fan before he could walk or talk. I made certain of
that. And over the next few years, I often took him to matches.
We occasionally saw Norwich play at Carrow Road or in the
Midlands. But I also took him to the City Ground to watch Forest. I would put him on the fence at the uncovered Bridgford
Road end and stand 15 yards back, with one eye on him and
one eye on the game. It was fine unless it rained.

Four years on from the Milk Cup final, we were once again
one more game away from Wembley. But our FA Cup semi-
final, against Everton at Villa Park, is now forgotten to history.
That afternoon in 1989, as graduate student at Harvard, I
was glued to my radio at 10am, US time, ready to listen to live
coverage of the semi-finals from the BBC World Service. But
excitement turned to tragedy, and ultimately travesty, as I
listened to the commentary while the Hillsborough catastrophe
unfolded. Sat alone that day, thousands of miles from home,
numbed with shock, I was transported back to the terraces, in
my case halfway up the Bridgford Road end having put my little
brother on the fence. It could have been any of us.

I returned from the US in 1990 to work at the *Financial Times* and live in North London, just half a mile from Highbury. And in 1992, we managed to get tickets to see Norwich visit Arsenal for the opening game of the first ever Premier League season. We were 2-0 down when, just before the hour mark, manager Mike Walker sent on our new signing, a graduate of the Manchester United academy, Mark Robins. The tickets we'd been able to get were in the Arsenal crowd, but given the state of the game, we felt relatively relaxed about celebrating when Robins scored what looked like a consolation, and the locals didn't mind too much. By the time Norwich went 3-2 up five minutes later, the atmosphere around us had become pretty frosty, and when Robins got his second to seal the victory, it was decidedly hostile. As the expletives rained down, the three of us sat very still, arms down, quietly humming 'On the Ball City' to ourselves.

That first Premier League season was brilliant for Norwich – and at last, Sky Sports meant that we could see it unfold regularly live on TV. Going into Christmas, City were top of the league and by the time Man United came to Carrow Road, live on Sky, on a Monday night in early April, we still had a chance of winning the title. That defeat was the moment when our championship-winning surge faltered, but we still finished third, and that huge footballing triumph gave Norwich the chance to put right a wrong.

Back in 1985, our Milk Cup victory over Sunderland should have meant a place in the UEFA Cup but the Heysel tragedy and subsequent ban of English teams from European competition denied Norwich that chance. Third place in the Premier League ended up securing us a UEFA Cup spot and a golden night in Munich which no Norwich fan – nor the history books – will ever forget.

For the next round, I managed to get a ticket in the River End for the home leg against Inter Milan. It was a magical evening. For years, as a boy I'd listened to European football on a small transistor radio that my parents had bought for my eighth birthday. I would lie in the dark, listening via an earpiece to the crackling commentary on Radio Two: electric atmospheres, exotic locations, great triumphs for Liverpool and Forest. But that night at Carrow Road, that same European football atmosphere crackled around me.

Dennis Bergkamp was brilliant, it was close, but we just lost out. And although the team did valiantly well in the return leg at the San Siro, it wasn't quite enough to pull things round. Twenty-one years on, we're still yet to qualify again for Euro-pean football – but it remains the ambition of every Norwich City fan who witnessed those glory nights. And we can still say with pride, as a result of Jeremy Goss' dynamite goal in Germany, that Norwich were the only English side to triumph over Bayern Munich at their old Olympic Stadium.

When I went to work for the Labour Party in 1994, I had to balance my work as an adviser to Gordon Brown with making time for football. But as often as I could, I would slip off to see Norwich play, in the evenings at London games, at Christmas or Easter in Norfolk or at away games near our home in Castle-ford in Yorkshire where Yvette, my wife, was now the Member of Parliament.

I saw Norwich play at Sheffield United, Sheffield Wednes-day, Barnsley, Burnley, Rotherham, Leeds, Grimsby and Hud-dersfield. One memorable game was against Sheffield Wednes-day in December 2001, which I went to with an old friend of mine Phil Webster. Then the Political Editor of *The Times*, Phil is Norfolk-born, a long-standing City fan and author of the official biography of Kevin Keelan, which he began researching while a young cub reporter on the *South Norfolk News*. Phil and I have been to many away games over the years, and that day at Hillsborough we saw Norwich win 5-0. I remember, though, that the shine was taken off our victory when the Tannoy announced that Ipswich had also won 5-0 that day.

Just as my time working for Gordon Brown here in the UK had a football tinge, so did our trips abroad. Four or five times a year we went to big international economic meetings in Washington DC. Luckily, the meetings normally started on Saturday afternoons, and the time difference meant we could take the Chancellor to important 'bilateral meetings' in a local bar in Virginia to see the Premiership games on TV. And when he really did have to make important bilateral phone calls, Gordon Brown would have to go and stand outside on the pavement to talk business with his French or American counterpart, so they couldn't hear the bar noise in the background.

It was in that bar that I sat on the phone, with my mum holding the other end of the line to Radio Norfolk, as I listened to hear whether Norwich would beat Stockport in 2002 and scrape into the Championship play-offs. And I was back on the phone the next day persuading my dad to go down to Carrow Road to queue for tickets. A week later, I was in the Upper Barclay watching Norwich emphatically beat Wolves 3-1 in the first leg, sealed by a memorable bullet header from Malky Mackay.

A couple of years before, the two local Norwich Members of Parliament, Ian Gibson and Charles Clarke, had formed a supporters group in Parliament – Canaries at Westminster – and asked me to be the treasurer and Phil Webster to be secretary. I don't think a minute was ever taken, a single pound was ever raised or any meeting ever chaired. But the Monday after the first leg, Ian Gibson rang the club to ask whether Canaries at Westminster might be able to purchase one away ticket for Molineux.

He succeeded and because Charles, Ian and Phil were going to be busy in Parliament, it was decided that I should be the group's envoy. That evening, the other three ran back and forth between a sports bar near Westminster and their duties in the House of Commons, while I filled in the gaps over the phone from Wolverhampton. The atmosphere was hugely intimidating. Wolves did manage to get one goal back, but I was able to ring back to Ian, Charles and Phil so they could hear the away fans singing as the final whistle blew.

The next day the quest for tickets began again for the final against Birmingham. By this time my parents were living out in Italy, while my younger brother was working for the *Financial Times* in New York. Andrew said he would fly back if I could get tickets – which, after ringing the club ticket line on repeat dial for two hours and a further hour on hold, I finally did. The atmosphere inside the Millennium Stadium, with the roof closed, was electric, with the most amazing bank of yellow and green around half of the stadium. It was more like a rock concert than a football match. Norwich battled hard all game and we lost on penalties after extra-time, but as we drove home on the M4 with our scarves still trailing out of the windows, it felt just like driving out of the Baseball Ground 25 years before, although this time without the police escort. We were confident our chance was going to come.

My parents moved back that summer from Italy to live in Aylmerton in North Norfolk and be close to my auntie Doreen and uncle Frank, who very sadly died of cancer soon after. We again fell into a pattern of arranging family get-togethers around football matches. And with Forest coming to Carrow Road on Boxing Day, and my brother-in-law, David, an avid Forest fan, we'd arranged to have a late Christmas lunch in the Gunn Club. Ten of us around a table next to the one where Delia Smith, her husband Michael and their family were having lunch. That day, it was announced that our loan star Darren Huckerby had signed on a permanent basis. We beat Forest 2-0, and the team never looked back.

Norwich were promoted to the Premier League and, with my brother, dad and his brother John Balls – father of the legendary *EDP* 'Fans-Eye View' columnist, my cousin Richard Balls – we had together bought two season tickets in the Upper Barclay. We saw some great clashes that season, but one game was, by far, the most memorable. We had continued our family pattern of meeting for lunch at the Gunn Club before games. We often saw Delia and Michael up there, and they invited me and my dad to be their guests for a game. My first ever match in the directors' box was the midweek game on Sky against Manchester City, just a few days after Norwich had come from 4-1 down to draw 4-4 at home to Middlesbrough.

This time it was Norwich who took a 2-0 lead but then Man City levelled by half-time. Delia turned to me on the front row of the directors' box and said 'they're not cheering anywhere near as loudly as they did against Middlesbrough, someone's got to tell them'. It was only after we had lost the game 3-2, and returned to the directors' lounge room, that we found out Delia had done just that, by popping out onto the pitch to tell the crowd 'let's be having you'.

At the time, everyone was rather taken aback by the scale of the TV and newspaper coverage. But when we arrived at Fulham for the final game of the season, needing to win to be sure of staying up, the *Eastern Daily Press* 'Let's be having you' centre-spread pull-out was ready on all our seats. Unfortunately City just didn't turn up that afternoon and we lost 6-0 – one of many miserable afternoons I have spent at Craven Cottage over the last decade. But 'let's be having you' has certainly entered football legend.

The next few seasons were pretty tough. Yvette stopped asking me on a Saturday afternoon, 'Did they win?' and instead asked, 'Did they lose again?' My only real Norwich City 'high' came when, as Secretary of State for Education, I was asked to draw the annual English Schools Cup. At my request, the FA agreed that we could do the draw using the traditional FA balls in the official sack. Not only that, but they were delivered to the department by Sir Trevor Brooking and a surprise guest, City legend Jeremy Goss. It's one of my most treasured pictures – me, Jeremy and Sir Trevor drawing out the FA balls and reading out the schools' names for the first round of the Minute Maid Cup.

Relegated to the third tier, beaten 7-1 by Colchester, we were at rock bottom in August 2009 when I got tickets for my brother and my eight-year old son, Joel, to see City play Hartlepool away. Joel only agreed to come if he could have a can of Coke on the way there and a hot dog at the game. Food-based bribery was vital at that stage of his City-supporting career. My brother was catching the train up from London to join us, and as he got into a cab to catch the train, the driver asked him where he was going and he replied, 'I'm going up to Hartlepool-Norwich'. The driver stopped the cab, turned round with a look of incredulity and said 'All that way? Are you in the team?'

But sitting just behind the dug-out in Hartlepool's tiddly ground, we could hear our new manager, Paul Lambert barking his orders and – with a 2-0 victory, the first away league win of the season – it was a turning point. While our recently appointed chairman and chief executive, Alan Bowkett and David McNally, together set about turning round the club's finances, Grant Holt – a great Bryan Gunn signing – went on to savage League One defences up and down the country.

During that season, my constituency boundaries changed and I became a Leeds Member of Parliament, with Elland Road just 100 yards down the road from the edge of my constituency. And the following year, with City back in the Championship, I made one of the biggest political mistakes of my career. Delia had suggested I come with them to an away game, and Leeds was obviously the most convenient option.

I arrived at the directors' lounge to be immediately berated by the then Leeds chairman, Ken Bates, about the cost of policing. I was sat next to Delia and Michael for the game, and when Leeds scored the first goal we stayed squarely in our seats as 29,000 Leeds fans stood up to cheer. But when Norwich equalised and as 2,000 Norwich fans in the away corner celebrated, thousands of Leeds fans neighbouring the directors' seats looked over to see a small group led by Delia Smith cheering and applauding and me, their local MP, the most jubilant of the lot.

As I sat down, I realised what a catastrophic mistake I'd made. From that moment, yelling and jeering directed at me from the nearby fans started and continued to the end of the game. With 10 minutes to go, the match was in the balance at 2-2 – and I am ashamed to admit, it is the only Norwich game I've ever been to where I was desperately hoping we wouldn't score a late winner because I was pretty sure that would have been me finished.

Promotion followed, even without those two extra points from Leeds. And then followed three brilliant, if at times hugely frustrating, seasons in the Premier League. The highs and lows are too many to recall, but included beating Arsenal and Man United at home, the 3-3 draw at the Emirates, beating QPR on New Year's Day at Loftus Road, terrible defeats against West Brom at home and Fulham away (again).

Relegation following Chris Hughton's departure was deeply disappointing, but for me there was one silver-lining. Travelling back from the defeat to Arsenal that confirmed our relegation my son turned to me and said, 'Dad, it's only when you lose at home and get relegated that you find out you're a true fan'. Never a truer word has been spoken. He's been a fanatic ever since.

I loved the Premier League. But, like many Norwich fans, I really enjoyed that 2014-15 season in the Championship, even if the first half was hugely frustrating. In January, I had invited Delia and Michael to come up to the House of Commons for dinner with Yvette and me to discuss politics, and beforehand they told me the club was about to make an announcement. I knew they had found Neil Adams' resignation very painful, but they said that, after a careful search, they were bringing in a young Scottish manager, Alex Neil. They were understandably nervous, but hopeful, given his promising track record.

What an inspired appointment it proved. The new manager turned things around with impressive speed. And from being 12 points off the play-offs in January we were challenging for automatic promotion. The crunch game was on a Friday night against Middlesbrough, with the 2015 General Election campaign already under way. I'd managed to secure the title of Labour's East of England Champion so that I could co-ordinate campaigning trips with home matches. It was a subtle strategy which nobody (other than BBC Look East, ITV Anglia and all my Labour colleagues) noticed.

That Friday we knocked on voters' doors in the city and then witnessed a very aggressive Middlesbrough team successfully kick Norwich off the pitch, with the referee a passive bystander.

That defeat meant we had to win promotion the hard way. With three days to go before the General Election I really didn't know what the future was going to hold for me, the country or the football club. Delia had come down to a final week election rally in Brighton and made a great speech. The polls were still neck and neck. All I knew for certain was that, two days after the General Election, Norwich were playing Ipswich at Portman Road in the first game of the play-offs.

If we'd won the election outright, which by that time seemed highly unlikely, I was definitely going to go to the first play-off game. If, as seemed much more realistic, there was a hung Parliament and a complex negotiation under way, I fully expected I wouldn't make the game. In the event, Labour lost the election outright and I lost my seat in the process.

Besieged by the media, we had to go into hiding. Joel and I ended up watching the Ipswich game on television from a friend's house. But the following Saturday we were back at Carrow Road for the second leg, with the tie finely balanced. We had a big family group – my son and younger daughter, Maddy, my dad, two uncles, my brother and his children, Jessie and Daniel, both mad fans who always seem to be wearing Norwich kit when not in school uniform. And together we witnessed one of Norwich's great victories.

We were off to Wembley again – that same family group, plus my godfather and mother-in-law too. My son and I were honoured to witness our emphatic victory from the Royal Box with Delia and Michael. Then afterwards we all went back to my brother's house to watch the whole game again on TV, joined by my mum, Yvette and our oldest daughter Ellie. Three different generations of our family, cousins, uncles all celebrating a great Norwich day.

So you see, Norwich City is where I come from. It shapes my earliest memories, it is the thread which links all the different phases of my life. It is at the core of a network of ties and experiences which unite my family through its multiple generations, just as it does for many thousands of other families, and many tens of thousands of supporters across the UK and around the world. I've met Norwich City supporters in Manchester, London, New York and Los Angeles, and visiting fans from the Netherlands, Finland and Australia. All part of that wider family.

I know, too, how important it is for Delia and Michael for

the board to be part of that wider family, with Norwich in the blood. In October after the General Election, I received an email from their office asking whether I could speak to them on the phone. I was put on the speaker phone on their dining room table. Delia explained that Stephen Fry was finding it impossible to balance his international work commitments and his NCFC commitments and that he was going to stand aside as a director and become a club ambassador instead. They asked whether I would be willing to join the Norwich City board as a non-executive director. Michael explained that they were also planning to bring onto the board their nephew, Tom Smith, who I already knew well as a deep, avid, and often highly vocal supporter.

A few months after losing my seat in Parliament, to be asked to do something that would never have been possible had I still been an MP was quite something. I said I was deeply honoured but thought I should sleep on it, before ringing my brother and Yvette who all said it was wonderful news.

The plan was to make the announcement in January. But a fortnight later, things changed. I was up for the Norwich home game against Everton as a guest of the club sponsor, Aviva. A couple of days before, I received an email from club chair Alan Bowkett. He'd been a hugely important servant to the club over six years, his financial acumen getting us through the dark days of 2009 when the club was really close to bankruptcy. But the email explained that, after six years, it was time for him to stand aside.

As I walked into the board room, Delia came over to me and said: 'I know you've heard the news and I know you've agreed to become a non-executive director, but would you mind stepping into the role of chair as well?' A minute later, Tom came over and said: 'Has Delia asked you yet? I do hope you're going to say yes'. This was quite a shock. It was one thing to become a non-executive director, quite another to become the chair with all the responsibility that entails. But it was literally for me the chance of a lifetime to serve the club I love, so I told Delia and Michael I was delighted to accept.

A whirlwind week later, I was sitting in a press conference before the Aston Villa game as my appointment was announced. It was only after that press conference, and after I'd posed for a photograph holding a Norwich scarf in the tunnel, that I realised quite what I was letting myself in for. Sat in the stands, as the game kicked off, I was hit by the rather obvious truth that there was absolutely nothing I could do at all to influence the course of events that afternoon – that was all going to happen out on the pitch. The nature of being the chair or director of a football club is that while you can make decisions which have an impact months or years ahead, the performance of the club day-to-day and week-to-week is totally out of your control.

If we'd lost to Aston Villa that day, it would have been a bad result for Norwich but a disastrous start for me – and I knew my Norfolk surname would have provided plenty of headline copy for the newspapers. Luckily we won – emphatically – and we went on to beat Southampton the following Saturday. If I'd resigned then, I would have been the most successful chair in Norwich City's history!

What a rollercoaster the rest of that 2015-16 season turned out to be. We had some good wins, at home to Newcastle and away at West Brom. We had some unlucky breaks, not least at home to Chelsea, but also some difficult and tumultuous afternoons – that 4-5 home defeat to Liverpool left me scarred for life. Relegation was a great disappointment, and David McNally's surprise resignation, after seven years' service, made my life much busier as we managed the summer transfer window and recruited a successor, the vastly experienced and highly respected former chief executive of Wolves, Jez Moxley.

My abiding memory of that season, though, will be the amazing way the City home crowd responded to the reality of relegation, despite beating Watford 4-2, as Sunderland's victory sealed our fate. The chants for manager Alex Neil, the singing echoing around from stand to stand, the anticipation of Ipswich derbies to come – it was a sight and sound that took the breath away and brought home to me what a special club we all support and what a great honour it is to do this job.

Of course, my role is, by definition, transitory. There have been past chairmen, and there will be future chairs. The same applies, of course, to players and managers, sponsors and directors. What is striking about Norwich City is that, while individuals come and go, the club's core values don't change. It is, and I hope always will be, a family club, a community club, run by fans of the club.

I never met either of my Norfolk grandfathers. My dad's father passed away when he was just ten years old, my mum's when she was 16. But walking to Carrow Road before a game, my dad would often talk to me about how his father, a lorry driver for the local gas company, would walk down Gas Hill on a Saturday morning after his shift, earn some more money for the family working on the turnstiles at Norwich City, then get the bus to the speedway in the evening to do his third job of the day as a steward there. My family was supporting Norwich City long before I was on this earth, and I'd like to think I've done a good job passing the passion on to the next generation.

My son, Joel, now comes to every game; our younger daughter has been to a few, I've even managed to get Yvette along to a game (my oldest daughter is work in progress). We've all regularly met up the night before games at my mum and dad's house close to the cathedral with my brother, his kids, and sometimes my sister and her family too.

One consequence of becoming chair of the football club is that I have been able to see my mum and dad much more than when I was in politics; which is very important to me. Norwich City has shaped my life now for close to five decades and my family's for much longer. And just like for so many other Norfolk and Norwich City supporting families, I know it will for many decades to come.

Ed Balls was an MP for a decade, held two cabinet posts and – most importantly – was a founder member of the four-strong 'Canaries in Westminster' group. At least four generations of his family were or are Norwich City supporters and he became the club chairman in December 2015. He is a Senior Fellow at Harvard and a visiting Professor of King's College, London.

ACKNOWLEDGEMENTS

My grateful thanks to Ian Thornton, director of the wonderful Norwich City Community Sports Foundation, who facilitated several of the meetings that led to chapters in this book. And a life-time's gratitude to my wife, Sarah, whose support with this project, particularly during a period when I was unwell, was 'just' what she's done, throughout our long love affair, whenever I have tackled anything.

Mick Dennis

DID YOU MISS VOLUME ONE OF TALES FROM THE CITY?

Have you got *Tales From The City Volume One* in your collection? These are the timeless stories it contains:

Bryan Gunn lays bare his soul about stepping forward to be manager after 22 years as a City man. And he discloses a secret.

Michael Wynn Jones, the fan who became an owner, gives an insider's account of some turbulent years at Carrow Road.

Iwan Roberts admits how he struggled with form and fitness before turning boos into cheers and becoming one of the club's all-time greats.

Charlie Wyett, the Hunstanton lad who became a top name on *The Sun*, reveals how different Norwich managers have handled the media.

Song-writer, blogger and YouTube star **Jon Rogers** explains why his relationship with the club has seldom gone to plan. Funny but poignant.

Novelist and scriptwriter **Lilie Ferrari** reports the story of the club's mascot, Captain Canary, and along the way gives a social history of the club.

Sky Sports presenter **Simon Thomas** takes the reader to the pitch-side at Wembley for a game that tested his professionalism.

Paul McVeigh tells a tale of persistent refusal to be floored by life's knocks. One game changed his life.

Radio Norfolk's lead commentator **Chris Goreham** recounts what it was like when his friend and colleague became City's manager.

Grant Holt, the man who led from the front as City charged up the divisions, takes us behind the scenes of that epic era.

A City manager criticised **Mick Dennis** at first but then helped him begin a career in football journalism.

TALES FROM THE
CITY

VOLUME THREE RELEASE DATE
TO BE ANNOUNCED